First World War
and Army of Occupation
War Diary
France, Belgium and Germany

38 DIVISION
Divisional Troops
119 Brigade Royal Field Artillery
22 December 1915 - 28 February 1917

WO95/2546/1

The Naval & Military Press Ltd
www.nmarchive.com
Published in association with The National Archives

Published by

The Naval & Military Press Ltd

Unit 10 Ridgewood Industrial Park,

Uckfield, East Sussex,

TN22 5QE England

Tel: +44 (0) 1825 749494

www.naval-military-press.com

www.nmarchive.com

This diary has been reprinted in facsimile from the original. Any imperfections are inevitably reproduced and the quality may fall short of modern type and cartographic standards.

© **Crown Copyright**
Images reproduced by permission of The National Archives, London, England, 2015.

Contents

Document type	Place/Title	Date From	Date To
Heading	WO95/2546/1		
Heading	38th Div 119th Bde. R.F.A. Vol: I		
War Diary	Pont Noyelles	01/01/1919	01/01/1919
War Diary	Southampton	22/12/1915	22/12/1915
War Diary	Havre	23/12/1915	23/12/1915
War Diary	St Venant	25/12/1915	01/07/1916
Miscellaneous	Lambres	01/06/1916	01/06/1916
War Diary	Pont Riqueul	02/06/1916	02/06/1916
War Diary	(Near) Laventie M, 12, A.	03/06/1916	13/06/1916
Heading	119th Bde: R.F.A. Vol 2		
Heading	119th Bde: R.F.A. Vol. 3		
War Diary	St Venant	12/01/1916	26/01/1916
War Diary	Vieille Chapelle	29/01/1916	31/01/1916
Heading	War Diary of 119th Brigade R.F.A. from Sat. Jan 1st to Monday. Jan 31st 1916. Volume I		
War Diary	Locon	15/02/1916	29/02/1916
War Diary	Brielen	23/09/1916	30/09/1916
Heading	War Diary of 119th Brigade R.F.A. from 1.2.1916 To 29.2.1916		
Miscellaneous		15/02/1916	15/02/1916
Heading	119 R F A Vol 4		
War Diary	Festubert	20/03/1916	21/03/1916
Heading	War Diary of 119th Brigade R.F.A. for March 1916 Vol 4		
War Diary	Locon	05/03/1916	21/03/1916
War Diary	France	01/03/1916	09/03/1916
War Diary	X 24 a 0.1	01/03/1916	31/03/1916
War Diary	Festubert Cuinchy Right Section Guns (F12.d)	07/03/1916	31/03/1916
Miscellaneous	119th Brigade Headquarters-M.4.b.3.4	16/04/1916	16/04/1916
War Diary	Locon	01/04/1916	15/04/1916
War Diary	Levantie	16/04/1916	06/05/1916
Operation(al) Order(s)	Operation Order No. 1, By Lieut., Col., P.J. Patterson D.S.O., R.F.A., Commanding Left Group R.F.A., 38th Divisional Artillery, (W.A.C.).	07/05/1916	07/05/1916
War Diary	Levantie.	06/05/1916	12/05/1916
Operation(al) Order(s)	Continuation of Operation Order No 2, By Lieut., Col., P.J. Paterson D.S.O., R.F.A., Commanding Left Group R.F.A., 38 D.A.	09/05/1916	09/05/1916
Operation(al) Order(s)	Operation Order No 2, By Lieut., Col., P.J. Patterson D.S.O., R.F.A., Commanding Left Group R.F.A., 38th Divisional Artillery (W.A.C.).	09/05/1916	09/05/1916
War Diary	Levantie	13/05/1916	24/05/1916
Miscellaneous	Scheme For Breaching Wyck Salient: Issued By Lieut., Col., P.J. Paterson D.S.O., R.F.A., Commanding Left Group R.F.A., 38th D.A.	13/05/1916	13/05/1916
War Diary	Levantie	24/05/1916	30/05/1916
Operation(al) Order(s)	Operation Order No. 3, By Lieut., Col., P.J. Paterson D.S.O., RFA., Commanding Left Group R.F.A., 38th Divisional Artillery, (W.A.C.)	26/05/1916	26/05/1916
War Diary	Levantie	31/05/1916	31/05/1916

Miscellaneous			
Heading	War Diary 119th Brigade R.F.A. from 1.6.16 to 30.6.16		
War Diary	Levantie	01/06/1916	12/06/1916
War Diary	St. Venant	13/06/1916	14/06/1916
War Diary	Marest	15/06/1916	15/06/1916
War Diary	St Michel	16/06/1916	27/06/1916
War Diary	Hardinval	28/06/1916	30/06/1916
Operation(al) Order(s)	Operation Order No. 5, By Lieut., Col., P.J. Paterson D.S.O., R.F.A., Commanding Left Group R.F.A., 38th Divisional Artillery, (W.A.C).	02/06/1916	02/06/1916
Operation(al) Order(s)	Operation Order No 7. By Lieut., Col., P.J. Paterson D.S.O., R.F.A. Commanding Left Group R.F.A. 38th D.A. (W.A.C.).	03/06/1916	03/06/1916
Operation(al) Order(s)	Operation Order No 6. By Lieut., Col., P.J. Paterson D.S.O., R.F.A. Commanding Left Group R.F.A. 38th D.A. (W.A.C.).	03/06/1916	03/06/1916
Heading	War Diary 119th Brigade R.F.A. Month of May 1916		
Operation(al) Order(s)	Operation Order No. 4, By Lieut., Col., P.J. Paterson D.S.O., R.F.A., Commanding Left Group R.F.A., 38th Divisional Artillery, (W.A.C.).	29/05/1916	29/05/1916
Heading	38th Div. XV. Corps. Division Transferred from II. Corps, Fourth Army, 3.7.16. Headquarters, 119th Brigade, R.F.A. July 1916		
War Diary	Mirvaux	01/07/1916	01/07/1916
War Diary	Harponville	02/07/1916	03/07/1916
War Diary	Treuxwood	04/07/1916	08/07/1916
War Diary	Fricourt	09/07/1916	19/07/1916
War Diary	St. Leger	20/07/1916	24/07/1916
War Diary	Mailly	25/07/1916	31/07/1916
War Diary	In front of Serre	20/07/1916	29/07/1916
War Diary	Couin	20/07/1916	25/07/1916
War Diary	Colincamps Wagon Line at St. Leger	20/07/1916	25/07/1916
War Diary	Colincamps	26/07/1916	31/07/1916
War Diary	Mailly Maillet	01/08/1916	08/08/1916
War Diary	Thievres	09/08/1916	09/08/1916
War Diary	Hem	10/08/1916	12/08/1916
War Diary	Zeggers-Cappel	13/08/1916	20/08/1916
War Diary	Trois Tours	21/08/1916	31/08/1916
Heading	War Diary of C Battery 119th Brigade R.F.A. from 1st August 1916 to 9th August 1916		
Heading	War Diary 119th Brigade R.F.A. Month of August 1916		
War Diary	K 21a 1.1 Sheet 57D	01/08/1916	01/08/1916
War Diary	Battery Position	02/08/1916	08/08/1916
War Diary	Collincamps (Supporting 20th Div Inf.)	01/08/1916	06/08/1916
War Diary	St Leger	07/08/1916	07/08/1916
War Diary	Thievres	08/08/1916	09/08/1916
War Diary	Trois Tours	01/09/1916	22/09/1916
War Diary	Proven	23/09/1916	28/09/1916
War Diary	Regersburg	29/09/1916	29/09/1916
Miscellaneous			
War Diary	Brielen FM. B 28 B8.6	23/09/1916	30/09/1916
War Diary	B 22d 1-8	23/09/1916	23/09/1916
War Diary	Dawson's Corner	26/09/1916	26/09/1916
War Diary	Sheet St Julien 1/10000	28/09/1916	29/09/1916
War Diary	In the Field Brielen.	23/09/1916	30/09/1916

Type	Description	Start	End
Operation(al) Order(s)	Operation Order No. 1 By Lieut., Col., P.J. Paterson D.S.O., R.F.A., Commanding Right Group R.F.A., 38th Div., Artillery.	09/10/1916	09/10/1916
Operation(al) Order(s)	Operation Order No. 2 By Lieut., Col., P.J. Paterson D.S.O., R.F.A., Commanding Right Group R.F.A., 38th Div., Artillery.	10/10/1916	10/10/1916
War Diary	Regersburg	01/10/1916	29/10/1916
War Diary	Hamhoek	30/10/1916	31/10/1916
War Diary	Dawson's Corner B 22d 1.8 Sheet 28	01/10/1916	30/10/1916
War Diary	Brielen B 28 B 8.6	01/10/1916	31/10/1916
War Diary	Ghent Cottages Brielen	01/10/1916	31/10/1916
War Diary	Hamhoek	01/11/1916	28/11/1916
War Diary	Troistours	29/11/1916	30/11/1916
War Diary	Dawsons Corner B 22d Sheet 28 NW	01/11/1916	27/11/1916
War Diary	Brielen B 28 B 8.6	01/11/1916	11/11/1916
War Diary	###		
War Diary	Herzeele	17/01/1917	17/01/1917
War Diary	Dawson's Corner B 22c-Sheet 28 N.W. 1/20000	18/01/1917	31/01/1917
War Diary	Brielen FM. B 28 B 8.6	18/01/1917	31/01/1917
War Diary	Battery H.Q at Ghent Cotts	17/01/1917	17/01/1917
War Diary	Brielen No 1 Gun in action at B.22.d 90 65 No 2 gun in open under Camouflage at B 22.d.25.4 c Left Section in pits built by Battery in Dec B.22.d.4.3	18/01/1917	18/01/1917
War Diary	O.P. Twin Cotts South B.17 b.7.3	19/01/1917	21/01/1917
War Diary	Battery H.Q.at Ghent Cotts	17/01/1917	17/01/1917
War Diary	Brielen No 1 gun in action at B.22.d. 90.65 No 2 gun in open under Camouflage at B.22.d.25.40 Left Section in pits built by Battery in Dec 16 B.22.d.4.3	18/01/1917	18/01/1917
War Diary	O.P Twin Cotts South B.17.b.7.3	19/01/1917	21/01/1917
War Diary	Brielen	22/01/1917	31/01/1917
War Diary	Brielen and Elverdinghe	01/02/1917	28/02/1917
War Diary	Ypres	03/02/1917	27/02/1917
War Diary	In the field	01/02/1917	27/02/1917
Miscellaneous	The following Should have been entered for January 26th 1917	26/01/1917	26/01/1917
War Diary	Elverdinghe	01/02/1917	28/02/1917

NC95/3546/1

119th Bde. R.F.A.
Vol: I

121/736

Dec '15

38th Div

… Army Form C. 2118.

WAR DIARY
or
INTELLIGENCE SUMMARY.

121 Bde RFA

Jan. 1919

Place	Date	Hour	Summary of Events and Information	Remarks and references to Appendices
PONT NOYELLES	Jan 1919. Jan 1.		Arrived in hutted Camp PONT NOYELLES, where the month was spent. Demobilization Dunn + hours continued.	

A.H. Parsh
Major RA
Cmdg. 121 Bde RFA.

Army Form C. 2118

WAR DIARY
or
INTELLIGENCE SUMMARY
(Erase heading not required.)

Place	Date	Hour	Summary of Events and Information	Remarks and references to Appendices
SOUTHAMPTON	22.12.15	5 pm	The 119th Brigade R.H.A., 38th D.A. (W.A.C.) left AVINGTON CAMP, WINCHESTER, December 22nd 1915; proceeded by route march to SOUTHAMPTON, where they embarked and sailed the same evening for HAVRE, FRANCE. List of officers :— Lieut. Col. P.J. PATERSON D.S.O. Commanding. Sgt. COOK W.D. Orderly. 2/Lieut. DEARLOVE Lieut. Orderly officer. Captain G.T. DORRELL V.C. Commanding "A" Battery. 2/Lieut. G.T.J. MORRIS. Ammn. officer. " " 2/Lieut. T.H. GRIFFITHS. Sec. Commander " " 2/Lieut. G.W. BELL Sec. Commander " " Major F.W. SALMOND. Commanding "B" Battery Lieut. J.E. RAMSLEY. Ammn. officer " " 2/Lieut. J.C. GRIFFITHS Sec. Commander " " 2/Lieut. M.K. JONES. Sec. Commander " " Captain R.W. DUFF. Commanding "C" Battery Lieut. F. DUPLOCK. Ammn. officer " " 2/Lieut. M.P. FITZGERALD Sec. Commander " " 2/Lieut. D.J. INGLETON. Sec. Commander " " Captain C.A.P. RHYS-PRYCE. Commanding "D" Battery 2/Lieut. T.J. JONES. Ammn. officer " " 2/Lieut. C.T. GIBSON Sec. Commander " " 2/Lieut. R.G. GRESLEY Sec. Commander " " Captain H. LEWIS. Commanding "B.A.C." Lieut. O.J. JONES (S.R.) Sec. Commander " " 2/Lt. R.M. WILKINSON JONES (S.R.) Sec. Commander " " 2/Lieut. E.R.F. STRACHAN Sec. Commander " " Lieut. W.B. LAURENCE Rame. (attached)	W.B.

Army Form C. 2118

WAR DIARY
or
INTELLIGENCE SUMMARY

(Erase heading not required.)

Instructions regarding War Diaries and Intelligence Summaries are contained in F.S. Regs., Part II. and the Staff Manual respectively. Title Pages will be prepared in manuscript.

Place	Date	Hour	Summary of Events and Information	Remarks and references to Appendices
HAVRE	23/12/1915	8 p.m.	On arrival at HAVRE in the morning of December 23rd the Brigade detrained and entrained at once for NORTHERN FRANCE	W.P.C.
ST VENANT	25/12/1915	6 p.m.	The Brigade detrained at LESTREM and arrived in billets near St VENANT in the early morning of December 25th 1915	W.P.C.
ST VENANT	30/12/1915	6 p.m.	Eight officers, twentyfour telephonists and ninetyfive N.C.Os and men of the Brigade left billets at noon on 31.12.1915 to join the Guards Brigade in the front line trenches for a course of instruction in the duties there	W.P.C.

W.P. Cook Lieut. R.F.A.
Adjt. for O.C. 119th Bde. R.F.A.

WAR DIARY or INTELLIGENCE SUMMARY

Army Form C. 2118

XXVIII A/119 RFA — June

Vol 1

Place	Date	Hour	Summary of Events and Information	Remarks and references to Appendices
	12/6/16		Battery marched from Lacoutie to Henneskerque.	
	13/6/16		Henneskerque to Mareot.	
	14/6/16		Mareot to Villers Bocton	
	15/6/16		Battery went into action at Neuville St Vaast relieving B/113 R.F.A.	
	28/6/16		Battery relieved by B/303 R.F.A. went out of action.	
	29/6/16 /30/6/16		Battery marched to Murawa - where it rejoined 119th Brigade R.F.A.	

Ryecroft
OC A/119 R.F.A.

C/119 RFA
Vol 1

Army Form C. 2118

WAR DIARY
or
INTELLIGENCE SUMMARY
(Erase heading not required.)

XXXVIII

Instructions regarding War Diaries and Intelligence Summaries are contained in F.S. Regs, Part II. and the Staff Manual respectively. Title Pages will be prepared in manuscript.

Place	Date	Hour	Summary of Events and Information	Remarks and references to Appendices
			References to Sheet 36 BELGIUM & FRANCE	
LAVENTIE S.	1.	9am	Marched via ESTAIRES and canal bank to MERVILLE to PONT RIQUEUL wagon line. Rest day. Amused April	
PONT RIQUEUL	2.	10am	B.C. & telephonists rode to position of B/120 (M12M) (1 mile south east of LAVENTIE) — a 2 gun position, intended to put in which Battery. Right Sec. came into action there at 3pm; gun emplacements not yet made. Enfilading trenches from DUCK'S BILL (Nunsta of BOIS du BIEZ) to BIRDCAGE (S of CHAPIGNY) (M24-2+) Range about 3200 to 4600. Shared O.P. with A/120. Out-observed chiefly from trenches	K.R.L. HUTLEY joined; posted from Base
(New)LAVENTIE M.12. A.	3.		Registered Rt. Sec. guns on zero line — a crossbeam in front line trench. Registered first from trenches	
	4.	2pm	Bombardment with T.M.s & harries of trenches south of BIRDCAGE; Coop'd. Fired 2 rounds.	
		11pm	Raid opposite BIRDCAGE. Stood by till 2am. Stormy day.	
	5.		B.C. inspected new O.P. at MOATED GRANGE; not yet completed.	
	6.		Little to relate. Gun emplacements for No. 3 & 4 guns completed.	
	7.			
	8.			
	9.			
	10.			
	11.			
	12.		Lft Section relieved by B/305 (61st Divn) and marched to ESTAVENANT for the night.	
	13.		R completed. Right Sec. marched 2nd & ST. VENANT. (inserted)	

J.R.Sligh, Capt RA
ami C/119 Bde R.F.A.

119th Bde: R.F.A.
Vol. 2

119th Bde: R.F.A.
Vol. 3

Army Form C. 2118.

WAR DIARY
or
INTELLIGENCE SUMMARY.
(Erase heading not required.)

Instructions regarding War Diaries and Intelligence Summaries are contained in F. S. Regs, Part II. and the Staff Manual respectively. Title pages will be prepared in manuscript.

Place	Date	Hour	Summary of Events and Information	Remarks and references to Appendices
ST VENANT	19.1.16		Captain R.W. DUFF admitted to Hospital sick.	WD@
ST VENANT	20.1.16		2nd Lieut. G. W. BELL admitted to Hospital sick.	WD@
ST VENANT	22.1.16	6 pm.	All officers and men attached to Guards Division returned to the Brigade.	WD@
ST VENANT	26.1.16	6 pm.	An advance party of one officer and twenty men from each Battery went today to be attached to 19th Divisional Artillery near VIELLE CHAPELLE.	WD@
VIELLE CHAPELLE			Captain H. LEWIS admitted to Hospital sick.	WD@
	29.1.16	6 pm.	One half the Brigade including personnel, horses and wagons proceeded to relieve an equal number of the 86th Brigade R.F.A. in action in place near VIELLE CHAPELLE.	WD@
VIELLE CHAPELLE	30.1.16	"	The remainder of the Brigade came up, and took over all the remainder of the Billets and Equipment of the 86th Brigade R.F.A.	WD@
VIELLE CHAPELLE	31.1.16	10 am.	The Brigade reported that they had completely taken over no to H.Q. R.F.A. 3rd Division. "A" Battery is acting as Counter Battery. "B" Battery has all its guns acting as Flank guns and attached to various other Batteries. "C" Battery has two guns attached to other Batteries as Flank guns. "D" Battery is attached to Left Group, 38th D.A.	WD@
"	31.1.16	6 p.m.	Officers joined during month, 2nd Lt C. Chollew Jany 15.16; 2nd Lt D. Lonergan Jany 18.16; 2nd Lt S. Nickols Jany 30.16.	WD@

W.D. Cook Lt
Captain, R.F.A.
Adjutant, 119th Brigade, R.F.A.

Confidential

War Diary of 119th
Brigade R.F.A.

from Sat. Jan. 1st
to
Monday. Jan 31st
1916.

Volume I

Army Form C. 2118

WAR DIARY
or
INTELLIGENCE SUMMARY
(Erase heading not required.)

Instructions regarding War Diaries and Intelligence Summaries are contained in F.S. Regs., Part II. and the Staff Manual respectively. Title Pages will be prepared in manuscript.

Place	Date	Hour	Summary of Events and Information	Remarks and references to Appendices
LOCON	15.2.16	6 p.m.	The whole Brigade remained in action, as reported on 31.1.1916 until the 14th to 15th when one half was withdrawn, and carried out the relief of the 2nd D.A. at a point between BETHUNE and LOCON	W390
LOCON	16.2.16	6 p.m.	The remainder of the Brigade continued the relief started on the 14th	W390
LOCON	18.2.16	6 p.m.	The Brigade reported as completely taking over the new positions "A" Battery acting as Counter Battery; "B" Battery attached to Centre Group; "C" Battery – one section as Counter Battery, and one section as Heavy Guns for Left Group; "D" Battery attached to Centre Group.	W390
LOCON	29.2.16	6 p.m.	Captain E.A. WOODS joined on 20.2.1916 Captain H. LEWIS, Captain R.W. DUFF and 2/Lieut. G.W. BELL, all evacuated to ENGLAND SICK. One Gunner of "B" Battery to Hospital – shell wound during the month.	W390

W. Cook Lt. 9 H A?
Lieut-Col. RA
Commanding H.gr. Bde R.H.A

WAR DIARY

~~INTELLIGENCE~~ SUMMARY

Army Form C. 2118

D/119/RFA

Place	Date	Hour	Summary of Events and Information	Remarks and references to Appendices
BRIELEN	Sept/13 1916		Lt. J.O. WILLIAMS went on Leave	
"	24		Capt. F.P. WYE attached R.A.H.Q as Brigade Major. Lt. W. ROBERTS returned from S'pdling Course.	
"	25		New night lines laid out for all guns orders of Group Commander.	
"	26		3 horses returned to M.V.S. in lieu of Bicycles received. Wool ahead now zippers with Buckall O.P. G.O.C.R.A. visited O.P.	
"	27		2nd Lt. W.O. HART 29th Div. Temp. attached to Battery. Registering all day for raid	
"	28	11.30 p.m.	Successful raid carried out on Front line trench. Barrage reported very good. 2/Lt Hart + N.C.O. observer shooting under instruction.	
"	29		Very dull misty all day.	
"	"	6 p.m.	Heavy shelling — T.M. on BOESINGHE.	
"	30		Very clear day registered many new targets. Hostile minenwerfers active during evening. Group called for retaliation.	

W. Roberts
2/Lt
D/119/RFA.

Confidential

War Diary of
119th Brigade R.F.A.

From 1·2·1916
To
29·2·1916

Volume 3

10/5

15.2.16

My dear Geddes,

Re your letter of yesterday. I was out on the 30th Div. front this afternoon & visited my batteries — all except the 121st which I hadn't time to — The 65th & 119th have had the hardest time but they are both perfectly happy & cheery & don't want any of their personnel relieved. They all want to see these operations out to an end, & I told them that was the right spirit. Of course though they are anxious to get back for a bit to straighten themselves out.

I am very glad they have done so well a little bit of praise bucks them up.

Yrs ever

A.H. Hussey

I fancy these batteries will be relieved very shortly anyway.

XXXVIII

119 RFA
Vol 4

Army Form C. 2118

WAR DIARY
or
INTELLIGENCE SUMMARY
(Erase heading not required.)

Place	Date	Hour	Summary of Events and Information	Remarks and references to Appendices
FESTUBERT	March 1916 20th-21st		Battery Position shelled. 90- 5.9" shells. No damage to personnel or Equipment. Vacated position that night. Moved into new position 800x further forward - just behind FESTUBERT.	

O'Rya Capt
OC. 21/19. R.F.A.

XXVIII

Confidential War Diary
of
119th Brigade R.F.A.
for
March 1916

Army Form C. 2118

WAR DIARY
or
INTELLIGENCE SUMMARY
(Erase heading not required.)

Instructions regarding War Diaries and Intelligence Summaries are contained in F.S. Regs., Part II. and the Staff Manual respectively. Title Pages will be prepared in manuscript.

Place	Date	Hour	Summary of Events and Information	Remarks and references to Appendices
LOCON	March 5/16		Major F. W. Salmond "B" Bty invalided to Eng.	WDSE
"	"	6 "	2 Lt C Challen "A" Bty wounded while attached to T.M. Bty.	WDSE
"	"	14 "	Captain Bligh joined the Brigade from 50 Brigade R.F.A.	WDSE
"	"	19 "	Lt W.D. Ross fulfilled the duties of Brigade Major R.A. and 2 Lt L. J. Dearlove resumed the duties of Adjt.	WDSE
"	"	20 "	D Bty shelled out of position, and took up an alternative position at x 30 C 6. 7 Lt Col P. J. Paterson proceeded on leave and Capt F. Y. Donnell V. D. assumed temporary command of the Brigade	WDSE
"	"	21 "	"C" Bty withdrew the 2 guns at Pont Logy M 34 C 5. 4 being relieved by "C" Bty 13-8th Brigade	WDSE

Malin
Lt Col Conway
119/R.F.A.

Army Form C. 2118

WAR DIARY
or
INTELLIGENCE SUMMARY
(Erase heading not required.)

Instructions regarding War Diaries and Intelligence Summaries are contained in F. S. Regs., Part II. and the Staff Manual respectively. Title Pages will be prepared in manuscript.

Place	Date	Hour	Summary of Events and Information	Remarks and references to Appendices
France	3/7/16		No change in position —	
	9/7/16		2 with T.C. Challon to field ambulance — forward with hand grenade striker attached to 380 Div. Trench mortar battery —	

Signed Bexly Pitt
O.in C. H.M. M7 mode.

WAR DIARY of B/119 BDE. R.F.A.

or

INTELLIGENCE SUMMARY

(Erase heading not required.)

Army Form C. 2118

Page (1)

Place	Date	Hour	Summary of Events and Information	Remarks and references to Appendices
X24a.0.1	1/3/16		Battery in action X24a.0.1 – Observing station at BREWERY S20 D 3.2 Waggon line at N16 D 4.7 –	Ref. 1/20000 Ed. 6. Sheet 36SE & 36 SW.
		1.30pm	Engaged German 2nd Line S28 B.6.8 in retaliation at request of infantry –	
		2pm–4pm	Carried out registration – S28 B 5.3 – S29 d 4.9 – S29 B 6.0 – Redoubt S28B78	
			Total rounds fired 65 – no casualties.	eaw.
— " —	2.3.16	12.35pm	Fired on enemy dias in German trench S28 B 6.6.	
		12.50pm	Registered farm S29 d 5.3.	
		1.30pm	Fired on houses S29d by order of CENTRE GROUP S29 no	
		2.30pm	Registered house at Xroads S24c 3.0.	
		3.45pm	Fired in retaliation at German and dias S22 B 4.3 – German artillery more active than	
			Total rounds fired 67 – no casualties.	eaw.
— " —	3.3.16	12.30pm	Fired in retaliation on German trench S22 d 4.3	
		1.30pm	And at movement on X road S24 c 3.0.	
		2.15pm	In trench S22 D 4.8	
			Total rounds fired 31 – 2 casualties	eaw.
— " —	4.3.16	4.30pm	Fired in retaliation on house S29d 4.8.	
		5.10pm	Dispersed working party S28 B 10.5.	
			Snow interfered with shooting observation – German artillery very quiet — no casualties	
			Total rounds fired 11 – no casualties	eaw.

WAR DIARY of B/119 BDE RFA
INTELLIGENCE SUMMARY
(Erase heading not required.)

Army Form C. 2118

Page 2

Instructions regarding War Diaries and Intelligence Summaries are contained in F.S. Regs., Part II. and the Staff Manual respectively. Title Pages will be prepared in manuscript.

Place	Date	Hour	Summary of Events and Information	Remarks and references to Appendices
X24a6.1	5.3.16	10.45am -11.45am	Fired on suspected O.P. in house S23d6.5 — House destroyed.	Ref from 20700 Ed 6. Sheet 36A55 + 36 3W.
		1.45pm + 4.25pm	Fired at movement on road T19c73.	
		2.15pm	Carried out registration on houses at S29c8.0 + A5B6.1.	
		3pm	Retaliated on houses S29d4.7 for shelling of FESTUBERT. Total rounds fired 73 — no casualties —	8cvo.
	6.3.16	2.15pm	Engaged new German works S23a 0.7	
		4.50pm	Retaliated on houses in S29d. Total rounds fired 39 — no casualties	8cvo.
	7.3.16	1.45pm	Fired in retaliation at houses in S29d. Total rounds fired 12 — no casualties. Snow rendered observation impossible today	8cvo.
	8.3.16	2pm	Retaliated houses S29d.	
		2.15pm	Fired on suspected O.P. at x roads S24c.3.0.	
		3.10pm -3.35pm	Retaliated at request of infantry on common trench S22d 2.4. Total rounds fired 77 — no casualties	8cvo.
	9.3.16	2.25pm -2.30pm	Retaliated on houses S29D or 2nd line S22D4.3 & S29D5.5. Total rounds fired 24 — no casualties	8cvo.
	10.3.16	10.20am 11.15am	Fired in retaliation at 2nd line S22D4.3. Fired 6 salvos into houses S29D by order of C group. Total rounds fired 32 — no casualties	8cvo.

WAR DIARY of B/119 BDE. R.F.A.

INTELLIGENCE SUMMARY

Army Form C. 2118

Page 3

(Erase heading not required.)

Place	Date	Hour	Summary of Events and Information	Remarks and references to Appendices
X24a01	11.3.16	4.20pm	Fired 2 rounds for test — light very bad for observation. No casualties.	Ref 57000 Ed. 6 Ghud. 36A SE. & 36 SW. enw
	12.3.16	12.40pm	Fired on suspected O.P. at S29 a.0.5½	
		2pm	Fired on new work at S29 a.3.4	
		3.15pm	Fired on house & new work in trench S22 d.6.1.	
			Total rounds fired 58 – 20 casualties	
	13.3.16	2.15pm	Fired on suspected O.P. in house S24 c.3.0.	enw
		3.10pm	Fired in retaliation at request of infantry on houses in S29 d.	
		4pm	Fired on movement in farm T19 c.7.3.	
		4.07pm	Fired on houses S29 d. in retaliation at request of infantry.	
		4.40pm	Searched for 2 A.A. guns observed firing from about T19 c.3.6	
			Total rounds fired 86 – no casualties	
	14.3.16	10.30am	Fired on suspected O.P. at S29 a.0.5½ in retaliation at request of infantry	enw
		11-12noon	Fired 20 rounds at strong point S28 B.111 by order of CENTRE GROUP.	
		12.45pm	Fired on Mamel at S22 c.9.5.	
		1.50pm	Fired on hut S22 B.61 at request of infantry	
		3pm	Dispersed working party at S24 d.8/6	
		3.20pm	Retaliated at request of infantry on houses S29 d	
		4-5pm	Fired 30 rounds by order of CENTRE GROUP at front + come S22 07.3.	enw
			Total rounds fired. 166 — no casualties	

WAR DIARY of B/119 Bde RFA

INTELLIGENCE SUMMARY

Army Form C. 2118

Page 4

(Erase heading not required.)

Place	Date	Hour	Summary of Events and Information	Remarks and references to Appendices
X24d61	15.3.16	4.45 pm	Fired 6 rounds on houses S29d in retaliation for request of infantry. No casualties	Ref 25000 Ed. 6 Sheets 36A S.G. 736 SW.
	16.3.16	1.10 pm	Fired on houses S29d at request of infantry	2do.
		3.40 pm 4.5.25 pm	Dispersed working parties at farm T19c7.3	
			Total rounds fired 30 — no casualties.	
	17.3.16	2.30 am	Fired on moving S22c 9.2.5 in conjunction with howitzers. By order of CENTRE GROUP.	
		5 pm	Registered mean night lines at S28a.9.4 + S22c.7.4	2do.
			Total rounds fired 34 — no casualties	
	18.3.16	1.15 pm	Dispersed working party T19c7.3.	
		5.15 pm	Searched for AA guns observed firing about T19c8.4	2do.
			Total rounds fired 10 — no casualties	
	19.3.16	12.20 1.15 pm	Fired on MOULIN D'EAU and German salient S22c at request of infantry on communication trench S22D	
		2.15 pm	Fired on movement at X roads 32YC.2.0.	
		4.45 4.5.15 pm	Fired in retaliation at request of infantry 42 — no casualties	2do.
			Total rounds fired 42 — no casualties	
	20.3.16	7.30 am 8.30 am 4.15 pm	Fired in retaliation at request of infantry at commn trench S22D	
		5.44 pm	Fired on O.P. at X roads S24C.8.0 by order — Total Rds fired 51 — No casualties	2do.

WAR DIARY of B/114 BDE. RFA.
INTELLIGENCE SUMMARY
(Erase heading not required.)

Army Form C. 2118
Page 5

Place	Date	Hour	Summary of Events and Information	Remarks and references to Appendices
Xa2 a.O.1	21.3.16		Did not fire — no hostile fire — no casualties	Ref Issue Bd. 6. S19.1.5 S8.4.5.5 or 56.5.w
	22.3.16		— " — German artillery very quiet. no casualties	ennw
	23.3.16		— " — no casualties	ennw
	24.3.16		— " — no hostile fire — no casualties	ennw
	25.3.16	12 noon	Retaliated at request of 16th RWF. O.P. common. trench S22.d — Total rounds fired 9 — no casualties	ennw
	26.3.16	8 am	Fired 4 rounds at a working party S22.c.6.1 — no casualties	ennw
	27.3.16		Did not fire — no casualties	ennw
	28.3.16	11.50 am	Fired at 3:0H1cm S24c 3.2 — Total rounds fired 3 — no casualties	ennw
	29.3.16	3.25 pm	Fired 2 rounds at Battery (Harris bridge) at T.19.C.3.6 — no casualties	ennw
	30.3.16	9.30 am 1.80 pm	Fired 12 Rds at suspected O.P. S29 d 4.5 by order of C' group. Fired on movement in house S29 d. — Total rounds fired 16 — no German answered at alternative position S19 a 3.8	ennw
	31.3.16	11.50 am 12.25 pm	Fired on common French S29 d in retaliation by order of C' group. O.P. S29 d 4.5	ennw
			Total rounds fired 20 — no casualties	ennw

Emmott
Capt RFA
Comdg B/114 Bde RFA

WAR DIARY
INTELLIGENCE SUMMARY
(Erase heading not required.)

Army Form C. 2118

Place	Date	Hour	Summary of Events and Information	Remarks and references to Appendices
			From 1st to 6th March inclusive Right section was attached to and in action with D/119, moving to an enfilade position, 400 yards North of BETHUNE — LA BASSEE canal on night of 1st.	
			From 1st to 20th March Left section was attached to C/157 Bde. in action near PONT LOGY (M.34.c. Sheet 36). For wire cutting, enfilading trenches S.16.a. and c. Wire cutting was carried out at S.10.d.2.6., working parties were fired on on several occasions at night. Fired about 16 rounds per day. Wire cutting 240 rounds at night.	Map squares. D.6.X. refer to Sheet 36 A. M.6.U. 36 D.6.L. 36 B A.19.A. 36 C
			From 20th to 31st March Left section was in rest at wagon line. Left section wagon line with B.A.C./119 at ECLUSE D'ESSARS (X.19.a) Right section wagon line D Bty 119 at LES GLATIGNIES (X.14.c)	

Army Form C. 2118

WAR DIARY
or
INTELLIGENCE SUMMARY
(Erase heading not required.)

Instructions regarding War Diaries and Intelligence Summaries are contained in F.S. Regs., Part II. and the Staff Manual respectively. Title Pages will be prepared in manuscript.

Place	Date March	Hour	Summary of Events and Information	Remarks and references to Appendices
FESTUBERT — CUINCHY Right Section gun (F.12.d.)			Map References to Sheet 36a. Squares P to X. Sheet 36B Squares D 5 L Sheet 36. " 36c " A to 1. " MSV.	
	7		Lightning bad. Showed at intervals. Otherwise quiet.	
	8		12 rounds 10 cm. How. fell near O.P at FESTUBERT. Fired 21 rounds at RUE D'OUVERT — registration.	
	9		Misty. Fired 30 rounds registering cross-road A.3. & 88. LE PLANTIN shelled by 10cm How.	9th Lt. WILKINSON JONES attached from Big 4th R.A.C. left on 23rd
	10		Misty. Fired 8 rounds at RUE D'OUVERT. (S.28.C.)	
	11		Quiet.	
	12		Misty till noon. Confined with How. on DOVER trench from S.27.d.8.8. to S.27.d.9.9, firing on wiring parties whenever they attempted to repair damage done to the parapet by their fire. (S.27.d.+28.a)	
	13	11-15am	Men seen behind RUE D'OUVERT. Fired 9 rounds.	
		2.4pm	Fired 11 rounds at cross roads S.28.c1.0.6. Clear day: enemy starvation balloons up	
	14	10am to 12noon	Enemy Field guns and trentgers very active in vicinity of FESTUBERT	14th Capt. J.F.BLIGH posted to Bty. Joined 23rd.
		2.30pm to 3pm	Fired 29 rounds at DOVER trench. Section of I Bty R.H.A near C/19 shelled by 10cm and 15cm hows. about 100 rounds.	
	15	3.65pm	FESTUBERT shelled with 10cm. Fired 27 rounds at DOVER trench: movement seen	
	16		Fired 6 rounds at RUE D'OUVERT. Considerable activity by hostile Artillery.	
	17		Misty. Very quiet. Fired 3 rounds on zero line. S.28.c.27.	
	18	11.50am	Fired 20 rounds at party moving near S.28.c.5.6. FESTUBERT shelled.	

Army Form C. 2118

WAR DIARY
or
INTELLIGENCE SUMMARY
(Erase heading not required.)

Instructions regarding War Diaries and Intelligence Summaries are contained in F.S. Regs., Part II. and the Staff Manual respectively. Title Pages will be prepared in manuscript.

Place	Date	Hour	Summary of Events and Information	Remarks and references to Appendices
	20	3.45pm to 5.40pm	DOVER trench from S.27.d.3.1 to S.28.a.3.4 Fired 102 rounds off in reply to urgent requests from Infantry for retaliation. Left section guns removed from front LOCns.	
	21.		Bad light. Quiet day.	
	22.		Misty: very quiet. No 1 guns removed for overhaul: No 3 from flat-top from wagon line to replace it.	
	23.		Misty. FESTUBERT shelled in morning by 10cm. howr. Snow at night.	
	24.		Snowed till 2pm. Little firing.	
	25.		Very good light in afternoon. Fired 16 rounds, registration; DOVER trench.	
	26.		Fired 10 rounds S.28.c.3.4. and S.27.d.9.9. Conference for officers at "C" Group HdQrs. 5pm	
	27.		Very wet evening. Further conference at "C" Group HdQrs.	
	28.		Fine. F.O.O in trenches at night. further registration of DOVER trench. 14 rounds.	
	29.		Dugout construction at gun position. Fired 10 rounds at DOVER trench, observed by F.O.O., in retaliation for shelling of our front line trenches.	
	30.		Fine and bright. Many German observation balloons up. FESTUBERT shelled.	
	31.		Very quiet. warm day.	

J.F.R____ Capt. R.F.A.
Comd. C/119 Bde. R.F.A.

119th BRIGADE HEADQUARTERS - M.4.b.3.4.

UNIT.	GUN POSITION.	WAGON LINE.
"A" Battery.	M.15.b.8.4.	G.27.d.8.5.
"B" Battery.	M.11.c.4.5.	G.26.d.7.1.
"C" Battery.	M.5.b.0.8.	G.27.b.7.4½.
"D" Battery.	M.6.a.9½.9½.	G.27.d.6.6.
"B.A.C."	-	G.20.d.0.1.

16.4.1916

119 RFA Vol 5

Army Form C. 2118.

WAR DIARY
or
INTELLIGENCE SUMMARY.
(Erase heading not required.)

XXXVIII

Hour, Date, Place	Summary of Events and Information	Remarks and references to Appendices
Locon 1.4.16.	Lt. Col. P.J. Fitzroy returned from leave, and resumed command of the Brigade. A very quiet day.	WDC
" 2.4.16.	A very fine bright day, nothing to report.	WDC
" 3.4.16.	Lt. Col. Patterson to WO with Adjt. & Lt. Deanbrie proceeded to Loisne to take over "C" troop, being the rear Staff of the 122nd Brigade.	WDC
" 4.4.16.	2 Lt. E.R. Atkins joined the Brigade and was posted to the Bde.	WDC
" 5.4.16	Lt. Duplock admitted to hospital owing to a fall from his horse.	WDC
" 6.4.16 to 9.4.16	Nothing to report.	WDC
" 13.4.16	Received orders to proceed to Laventie and take over the left group of the 38th Divn. on the 1st, Adjutant & Front move to be carried out and report to R.A. 38th Divn by 10 am 16.4.16.	WDC
" 14.4.16 15.4.16	Brigade moved by Rectons on the two days and took up positions in action new front. Copy of the positions attached.	WDC

Army Form C. 2118.

WAR DIARY
or
INTELLIGENCE SUMMARY.
(Erase heading not required.)

Hour, Date, Place	Summary of Events and Information	Remarks and references to Appendices
Zwartie 16.4.16	Mine reported to R.A. 38th Div. as complete. Very little movement in enemy lines "B" "C" "D" Btys carried out registration on new zones. Enemy shells very little with no effect	WDC
" 17.4.16	All Btys fired today mostly at enemy working parties. The enemy shelled various portions of our area without any effect. They shelled heavy slope to B.Btys gun position about 30 rounds of 77 m. Obtained one direct hit on a gun pit no damage done	WDC
" 18.4.16	Nothing unusual the enemy shelling and registration on both sides	WDC
" 19.4.16 to 21.4.16	Enemys artillery fairly active and aggressive. Shelled many places on our front without any result to men or material. Our retaliation was small, not seeming to shew up on a large scale.	WDC
" 22.4.16	Enemys artillery more aggressive fired 1. 2. 3 rounds at gun position of "D" Bty- 119 R.F.A. Obtained two direct hits on gun pits. No casualties, material damage very slight. May of the steel shell 5.9 in were blind.	WDC

Army Form C. 2118.

WAR DIARY
or
INTELLIGENCE SUMMARY.
(Erase heading not required.)

Instructions regarding War Diaries and Intelligence Summaries are contained in F.S. Regs., Part II. and the Staff Manual respectively. Title pages will be prepared in manuscript.

Hour, Date, Place	Summary of Events and Information	Remarks and references to Appendices
LEVANTIE. 23.4.16	Very little activity on either side.	W.D.C.
" 24.4.16	Enemy shelled various points in retaliation for our shelling their front line in conjunction with Registration of T. Mortars. No artillery dealings although they obtained several hits on O.Ps.	W.D.C.
" 25.4.16	Little activity on either side.	W.D.C.
" 26.4.16	Our Artillery fired a considerable number of rounds in conjunction with the Registration of T. Mortars. Drew heavy retaliation from enemy on our O.Ps. Several hits but no casualties.	W.D.C.
" 27.4.16	The enemy again shelled our O.Ps and obtained several direct hits on the Farm O.P. at N.13.a.5.3. slightly wounding two men.	W.D.C.
" 28.4.16	During the early morning the enemy shelled with T. Mortars on our front line and we retaliated with about 40 rounds firing Reared.	W.D.C.

Forms/C. 2118/10

Army Form C. 2118.

WAR DIARY
or
INTELLIGENCE SUMMARY.
(Erase heading not required.)

Hour, Date, Place	Summary of Events and Information	Remarks and references to Appendices
LE VANTIE. 29.4.16	Nothing special to report	WDC
" 30.4.16	All wagon lines and B.a.C. of this Brigade moved today to new locations at — "A" By. R. 10 c 48. "B" By. a t P. y d 1.2. "C" By. A. 16. a: 8.9: "D" By R. 10 a 4.8: B.a.C R. 11. a. 1.1. The ordinary retaliation on both sides.	WDC
	During the month 2/Lt J Dryhook was invalided to England sick through a fall from his horse. 2/Lt R Atkin joined. Reporting in 3.4.16. 2/Lt R.T. Gibson, and R.M. Wilkman Jones were admitted to hosp. sick.	WDC

M W [signature]
Lt Col R.A.
Comdg 119th Brigade R.F.A.

Map Sheets for
reference 1/10,000
36 a. S.E: 36 A.N.E.
36 S.W: 36 N.W:

119 Bde R.F.A.
R.F.A. 111

Army Form C. 2118.

WAR DIARY
or
INTELLIGENCE SUMMARY.
(Erase heading not required.)

Instructions regarding War Diaries and Intelligence Summaries are contained in F.S. Regs., Part II. and the Staff Manual respectively. Title pages will be prepared in manuscript.

Hour, Date, Place	Summary of Events and Information	Remarks and references to Appendices
LEVANTIE 1.5.16	Nothing out of the ordinary to report. Firing on both sides very light.	WDC
2.5.16	Enemy were a little more active today. The Neiwach or F.499'S.A.R.T. M24d36. was heavily shelled, with very little effect.	WDC
3.5.16	Incendiary shells were used today by the Enemy setting fire to several bivios in our area. The Battery of B/119. at the gun position was set on fire (M11©7.4.J. Slight material damage was caused to carriages etc to men. Not much other activity.	WDC
4.5.16	Enemy started shelling our position at D"104. with 5.9 Howgrs - about 7.30 am. Very slow at first - but increased in speed considerably at about 12 noon N-Ceased. No casualties.	WDC
5.5.16	Although some very close shooting. Both sides fairly quiet.	WDC
6.5.16	Enemy shelled a portion of our front line & communication trenches very heavily about N13.b. and N13.c. at 3am. We retaliated fifteen about 40 rounds of H.E. Shows	WDC

S E C R E T.

OPERATION ORDER NO. 1, BY LIEUT., COL., P.J.PATERSON D.S.O., R.F.A.,
COMMANDING LEFT GROUP, R.F.A., 38th DIVISIONAL ARTILLERY, (W.A.C.).

Map Reference - Sheet 36 S.W.1.

| Headquarters | Hendry | 7th May 1916. |

(1)   A raid is proposed to take place on the German line at N.14.c.7.4. at 12 midnight on the night of 7.5.1916.

(2)   All persons taking part in the raid will have their faces blacked.

(3)   2/Lieut., D.F.Ingleton will accompany the Raiding Officer, and will arrange to keep into communication with 2/Lieut., J.C. Griffiths, who will be in the front line trench, and in communication with the BERKLEY, BRISTOL and TEME B.S.

(4)   2/Lieut., D.F.Ingleton will arrange to have a flash signal and a runner for use in case the telephone line to 2/Lieut., J.C. Griffiths breaks down.

(5)   The following Batteries will stand to, and be ready to open fire at a moment's notice, on their respective targets, as allotted:-

Battery.	Target.
"C" / 119.	N.15.d.8.8; N.15.d.10.9; N.14.c.4.10; N.14.c.2.4.
"C" / 122.	N.15.d.5.5; N.15.d.15.5; N.15.d.3.8; N.14.c.2.10.
"D" / 119.	N.14.b.2.5; N.8.d.4.2; N.8.d.6].3; N.14.b.8.2.
"D" / 122.	N.14.b.2.3; N.8.d.4.8; N.8.d.6].5;

(6)   Should it be necessary to open fire to cover the withdrawal of the raiders, 2/Lieut. Ingleton, in consultation with the Raid Commander, will give the word "Strafe", to 2/Lieut., J.C.Griffiths, who will pass it on direct to Batteries concerned. These will immediately open with rounds of Battery fire, one sec. for one minute, after which they will slacken the rate of fire - firing bursts of fire as the situation seems to demand, as judged by the intensity of hostile fire. As a rough guide 100 rounds per 18pdr. Battery and 50 rounds per Howitzer Battery may suffice.

Lieut., R.F.A.
Adjutant., Left Group R.F.A.

Copy No. 1 Filed.
  "   " 2 to 113th Infantry Bde.
  "   " 3 "   38th Div.
  "   " 4 "D"/119.
  "   " 5 "D"/119.
  "   " 6 "C"/122.
  "   " 7 "C"/119.
  "   " 8 Captain Crow.
  "   " 9 2/Lieut.D.F.Ingleton.
  "   " 10 2/Lieut. J.C.Griffiths.
  "   " 11.War Diary
  "   " 12.War Diary

Army Form C. 2118.

WAR DIARY
or
INTELLIGENCE SUMMARY.
(Erase heading not required.)

Instructions regarding War Diaries and Intelligence Summaries are contained in F.S. Regs., Part II. and the Staff Manual respectively. Title pages will be prepared in manuscript.

Hour, Date, Place	Summary of Events and Information	Remarks and references to Appendices
LEVANTIE, 6.5.16 (Cont'd)	There were not many casualties	WDC
" 7.5.16	Very quiet throughout the day. A raid was organized and carried out successfully. Operation order for the Group arty attached. It was not necessary to open fire.	WDC
" 8.5.16	Small roving parties were fired on but much firing on little rise	WDC
" 9.5.16	A quiet day. Organization of another raid. Operation order attached.	WDC
" 10.5.16	Raid did not take place, so co-operation was not necessary. Our Bty fired very little during the day. Enemy artillery slightly active	WDC
" 11.5.16	"A" Bty gun position at M.15.b.8.4. was shelled by 4.2 and 5.9 Hows. No casualties to material. One sgt was slightly wounded in the chest from shell, but still at duty. Our Bty fired very little.	WDC
" 12.5.16	Nothing to report.	WDC

SECRET.   Copy No. 11

CONTINUATION OF OPERATION ORDER NO 2, BY LIEUT., COL., P.J.
PATERSON D.S.O., R.F.A., COMMANDING XXXXX LEFT GROUP R.F.A., 38 D.A.

Headquarters   Tuesday   May 9th 1916.

    In Continuation of No. 8 of above order, the time of the proposed raid will be any hour after 11.30 pm., 9th inst.

                                              W. Cook Lieut., R.F.A.
                                  Adjutant, Left Group R.F.A.

Copy No. 1 filed.
       2 113th Inf. Bde.
       3 R.A., 38th Div.
       4 A/119.
       5 B/119.
       6 C/122.
       7 Captain Thomas.
       8 2/Lt., G.T.J.Morris.
       9 2/Lt. L.J.Dearlove.
     10 War Diary.
     11 :   :

SECRET.   Copy No. 11

OPERATION ORDER NO. 2, BY LIEUT., COL., P.J.PATTISON D.S.O., R.F.A.
COMMANDING LEFT GROUP R.F.A., 36th DIVISIONAL ARTILLERY (U.A.C.).

Headquarters   Tuesday   8th May 1916.

(1)   A raid is proposed to take place on the German line at
         N.24.d.9½.6½. on the night of 9/10 May 1916.

(2)   All personnel taking part in the raid will have their faces and
         hands blacked.

(3)   2/Lieut., G.T.J.Norris will accompany the raiding officer
         and remain with him at a selected point until ordered to
         retire. He will be responsible for communications with the
         O.P.A.HOUSE, BARN and ST G. HOUSE.

(4)   2/Lieut., L.J.Bearlove will assist with all communications,
         both telephone and visual.

(5)   A signaller will accompany 2/Lt., G.T.J.Norris, also a
         runner, in case communications break down.

(6)   The following Batteries will stand to and be ready to open
         fire at a moments notice on their respective targets, as allotted:-

         Battery.   Targets.

         "A" Battery, 119 Bde.   WOOD C.b.0.0. and towards N.30.b.4.10.
                                       COMM(trenches N.19.c.2½.3.)
         "B" Battery, 119 Bde.   Selected points in TWELVT.
         "C" Battery, 122nd Brigade   N.19.a.3.6; N.19.c.5.3; N.19.a.3½.1;
                                       N.19.a.4.2.

(7)   Should it be necessary to open fire to cover the withdrawal
         of the raiders 2/Lieut., Norris, in consultation with the
         raid commander will give the word "Strafe" direct to Batteries
         concerned. These will immediately open with rounds of Battery
         fire, one sec, for one minute, after which they will slacken the
         rate of fire, - firing bursts of fire as the situation seems to
         demand as judged by the intensity of M.G. fire. As a rough guide
         100 rounds per 18 pdr. Battery and How. Battery may suffice.

(8)   Zero time will be notified later.

                                            W.D.Cook
                                            Lieut., C. F. A.
                                       Adjutant Left Group R. F. A.

Copy No. 1 Filed.
        2 112 Inf. Bde.
        3 R.A., 36th Div.
        4 A/119.
        5 B/119.
        6 C/122.
        7 Capt. Thomas.
        8 2/Lt. G.T.J. Norris.
        9 2/Lt. L.J. Bearlove.
       10 War Diary.
       11

Army Form C. 2118.

WAR DIARY
or
INTELLIGENCE SUMMARY.
(Erase heading not required.)

Instructions regarding War Diaries and Intelligence Summaries are contained in F. S. Regs., Part II. and the Staff Manual respectively. Title pages will be prepared in manuscript.

Place	Date	Hour	Summary of Events and Information	Remarks and references to Appendices
LEVANTIE	13.5.16		Very little done on either side.	WDC
"	14.5.16		Scheme for breaching of WYCK salient - drawn up. Copy attached.	WDC
"	15.5.16		The breaching of the WYCK salient was successfully carried out in conjunction with Heavies and T. mortars. Very small Artillery retaliation from the enemy	WDC
"	16.5.16		The enemy retaliated very heavily on our front line and O. Ps. to the shelling of the WYCK on the previous day. Very little damage was done. The reply was very vigorous.	WDC
"	17.5.16 / 18.5.16		Nothing to report.	WDC
"	19.5.16 / 20.5.16		Increased Artillery activity on both sides. Very little damage to our side. Principal enemy retaliation on O.Ps.	WDC
"	21.5.16 / 22.5.16 / 23.5.16		Quiet days. Small retaliation on both sides.	WDC
"	24.5.16		A considerable amount of firing was carried out by us on account of Germany shelling of our communication Trenches. A 119 Bde has become A 122 Bde. A 119 & Bde, A 122 Bde has become D 119. Bde. has been re-formed leaving 3-18 pdrs + 1 Howz. Bty in each F.A. Brigade.	WDC

1577. Wt. W2991/1773 500 2/15 D.D. & L. A.D.S.S./Forms/C. 2118.

SECRET.   Copy 6..........

SCHEME FOR BREACHING WYCK SALIENT : ISSUED BY LIEUT., COL., P. J.
PATERSON D.S.O., R.F.A., COMMANDING LEFT GROUP A.F.A., 38th D.A.

Headquarters   Sunday   28th May 1916.

(1)   Object is to breach WYCK Salient and enlarge the breach.
Operations will commence at zero time.

(2)   Trench Mortars will attack the flanks of the Salient –
N.15.d.5.7. and N.15.d.1a.5A. 72 rounds, at which is .A.3600.
        The fire of the Trench Mortars will be covered by "B"/122
Howitzer battery, covering the point of the Salient, and "A"/119
and "B"/119 enfilading the sides. Time allowed one hour.

(3)   The Howies are to engage the point of WYCK Salient, and
will make as wide a breach as possible; 60 rounds, time one hour.
These will commence at 0 – 1 hour.
        At 0 – 2 hours "B"/119 will fire for 40 minutes, to widen
breach.
        "A"/119 will be prepared to barrage at a moment's notice
from N.34.c.6.5. to N.15.c.8.1. in case of Hostile attack, and
also will, from the point of WYCK Salient to N.15.d.8.5.
        "B"/119 will be prepared to barrage at a moment's notice from
N.14.a.6.1. to N.8.d.5.5. in case of hostile attack.
        The Howitzer Battery, "B"/122 will also be prepared to
barrage.
        During the fire of the Howies the following batteries will
co-operate :–
        "C"/119 will enfilade WYCK Salient to N.14.c.4.5. – 10 rds.
        "C"/119 will enfilade W.Co. Trench – N.34.c.a.4. – 10 rds.
        "B"/119 will enfilade trench N.14.c.5.5. to N.14.c.6.2.
                  – 10 rounds; Point of WYCK Salient to N.15.a.4.5.
                  – 10 rds.

(4)   "B"/119 will keep guard on WYCK during the night after
the bombardment, and will open fire if called upon by the
Infantry.

                                    J Bradley 2/Lieut., R. F. A.
                                    a/Adjutant Left Group R. F. A.

Copy No. 1 Filed.
      2 115th Inf. Bde.
      3 R.A. 38th Div.
      4 "A"/119.
      5 "B"/119.
      6 "C"/119.
      7 "D"/119.
      8 "B"/122.
      9 "B"/122.
     10 "C"/122.
     11 War Diary.
     12 " "

Army Form C. 2118.

WAR DIARY
or
INTELLIGENCE SUMMARY.
(Erase heading not required.)

Instructions regarding War Diaries and Intelligence Summaries are contained in F. S. Regs., Part II. and the Staff Manual respectively. Title pages will be prepared in manuscript.

Place	Date	Hour	Summary of Events and Information	Remarks and references to Appendices
LEVANTIE	24.5.16		"C" Bty. 119th Brigade was withdrawn from the line on 23.5./16 and sent for training in field movements at Airs. The Res. 119th Brigade ceased to exist as a unit from 21.5.16. All Officers, N.C.Os. men, Horses, wagons etc being sent to the D.A.C. for transfer to the Base, where not required.	WDC
"	25.5.16 to 26.5.16		Nothing to report	WDC
"	27.5.16		A scheme for breaking the enemy parapet by attached was successfully carried out in conjunction with T. Mortars and Howitzers. Considerable damage was done to the parapet at the point, and the enemy wire much broken up.	WDC
"	28.5.16		Very quiet day	WDC
"	29.5.16		Very little doing on either side. "D" 119/R.F.A. had one man wounded, with a bullet, probably from a machine gun.	WDC
"	30.5.16		During the night from 9 to 10 p.m. considerable shooting on our left induced a certain amount of retaliation from our Btys. the F.A.R.M.O.P. was struck twice by 5.9 but no casualties to men.	WDC

SECRET.   Order No. 9

OPERATION ORDER NO. 3, BY LIEUT., COL., P.J.PATERSON D.S.O.,RFA.,
COMMANDING LEFT GROUP R.F.A., 38th DIVISIONAL ARTILLERY, (W.A.C.)

<u>Headquarters</u>   <u>Friday</u>   26th May 1916.

(1)   Intention is to breach front and support parapet and wire at N.19.a.3.5. by Trench Mortars, on the 27th May 1916.

(2)   "A"/122)
        "D"/122) will co-operate in covering the registration of Trench Mortars and completing the breach after the Trench Mortars have completed their shoot should the latter not succeed in making a breach. During the time the Trench Mortars are registering and firing, "A"/122 will engage the enemy's parapet on each flank of the proposed breach, to keep the enemy's heads down.

(3)   The registration of Trench Mortars will commence at 12 noon.

(4)   Officers Commanding the two Batteries concerned, will meet Lieut., O. J. Jones at the C.R.A., O.P. at 11.15 am., 27.5.1916.

(5)   The O.C. "A"/122 will arrange telephonic and visual communication from C.R.A. HOUSE to our trenches, opposite point to be breached.

(6)   The Group Commander will be at C.R.A HOUSE at 11.15am.

                                            Lieut., R. F. A.
                                     Adjutant Left Group R. F. A.

Copy No. 1 Filed.
        2 R.A., 38th Div.
        3 114th Inf. Bde.
        4 "A"/122.
        5 "D"/122.
        6 Lieut., O.J.Jones.
        7 War Diary.
        8

Army Form C. 2118.

WAR DIARY
or
INTELLIGENCE SUMMARY.
(Erase heading not required.)

Place	Date	Hour	Summary of Events and Information	Remarks and references to Appendices
LEVANTIE	31.5.16		A shoot was carried out by one of our B'ty's in conjunction with T. Mortars on Enemy Parapet at- SW 13 a 5.7. It was fairly successful knocking the parapet about in several places. (Copy of Order attached). A fair amount of Retaliation occurred after the shoot. Map Reference. Sheet 36 S.W.I. Ed. 6.	W.D.O.

M[signature]
Lt Col R.H.A.
Comdg. 119th Brigade R.F.A.
31.5.16

Army Form C. 2118.

WAR DIARY
or
INTELLIGENCE SUMMARY.
(Erase heading not required.)

Instructions regarding War Diaries and Intelligence Summaries are contained in F. S. Regs., Part II. and the Staff Manual respectively. Title pages will be prepared in manuscript.

Place	Date	Hour	Summary of Events and Information	Remarks and references to Appendices

1577 Wt.W10791/1773 500,000 1/15 D. D. & L. A.D.S.S./Forms/C. 2118.

Confidential

WAR DIARY.
119th Brigade R.F.A.
From 1.6.16. to 30.6.16.

WAR DIARY or INTELLIGENCE SUMMARY

Army Form C. 2118.

119 RFA XXXVIII Vol 7

June

Place	Date	Hour	Summary of Events and Information	Remarks and references to Appendices
LEVANTIE	1.6.16		C/119. R.F.A. returned from training at Airs, and went into billets at waggon line at R.1.D C D.4. (Sheet 36A) Scarcely any firing today	W.D.C
"	2.6.16.		One sec. of C/119 went into action in the Right Group R.F.A at M.12 a P.1.10 relieving one section of B/120. Considerable activity on our D.Ps. by 5.9" + 4.2's	W.D.C
"	3.6.16.		A Co-operation scheme was carried out with Trench mortars. Copy of order attached.	W.D.C
"	4.6.16.		A copy of orders for two raids attached. The raids were carried out. Our Btys fired on per orders. Enemy retaliated. No casualties	W.D.C
"	5.6.16 to 10.6.16.		Nothing occurred except the usual retaliation on both sides.	W.D.C
"	11.6.16.		Orders have been received to withdraw from the line by sections commencing tonight - A/119 being relieved by C/174. and B/119 being relieved by B/30. Relief carried out in night - one sec of each Bty. being back to waggon line & thence to ST VENANT at J 29 c 8.3. and J 29 d 4.2 respectively Sheet 36 H.	W.D.C

Army Form C. 2118.

WAR DIARY
or
INTELLIGENCE SUMMARY.
(Erase heading not required.)

Instructions regarding War Diaries and Intelligence Summaries are contained in F.S. Regs., Part II. and the Staff Manual respectively. Title pages will be prepared in manuscript.

Place	Date	Hour	Summary of Events and Information	Remarks and references to Appendices
LAVANTIE	12.6.16		Reliefs as ordered carried out. also first section of "C" + "D" Btys relieved in Right. Section and Wagon Lines moved to St VENANT	WDSC
ST. VENANT	13.6.16		Remaining Btys moved back to ST VENANT also Bde Hdqrs. "A" & "B" Btys marched from ST VENANT to take up position in the line north of ARRAS in 3rd Army Area under charge of 51st Divn.	WDSC
"	14.6.16		Rest for troops in ST VENANT.	WDSC
MAREST	15.6.16		Bde Hdqrs and C & D Btys marched by road by LILLERS to MAREST and halted in billets for the night.	WDSC
St MICHEL	16.6.16		Arrived in camp at ST MICHEL (3rd Army Training Area)	WDSC
"	17.6.16 to 22.6.16		Bty training, signalling & laying carried out	WDSC
"	23.6.16 to 24.6.16		Field movements and bivouacing at night practiced.	WDSC
"	25.6.16		Divisional field day practice at close support of Infantry.	WDSC

Army Form C. 2118.

WAR DIARY
or
INTELLIGENCE SUMMARY.
(Erase heading not required.)

Instructions regarding War Diaries and Intelligence Summaries are contained in F. S. Regs., Part II. and the Staff Manual respectively. Title pages will be prepared in manuscript.

Place	Date	Hour	Summary of Events and Information	Remarks and references to Appendices
ST MICHEL	26.6.16		Rest	WDP. WDP
ST MICHEL	27.6.16		Started march to HARDINVAL at 6.30 pm	WDP
HARDINVAL	28.6.16		Arrived at 1.15 am rested during the day	WDP WDP
"	29.6.16		Nothing to report	WDP
"	30.6.16		Started march to MIRVAUX at 9 pm	
			Map reference Sheet Serie II. 36a Hazebrouck	
			1.7.16.	

Mew
Lt Col R.H.A.
Comdg 119th Brigade R.H.A.

SECRET.   Order No. 8

OPERATION ORDER NO. 5, BY LIEUT., COL., P.J.PATERSON D.S.O., R.F.A.,
COMMANDING LEFT GROUP R.F.A., 38th DIVISIONAL ARTILLERY, (W.A.C.).

Headquarters   Friday   2nd June 1916.

Map reference Sheet 36 S.W.P, Edn. 6.

(1)   Intention is to breach front and support parapet and wire
at N.14.a.5.0. by trench mortars on 3.6.1916.

(2)   "A"/121 and "C"/121, 18 pdr. Batteries, will co-operate in
covering the registration of Trench Mortars.   During the time
the Trench Mortars are registering, both Batteries will engage the
parapet to keep the enemy's heads down.

(~~3~~)   ~~Batteries will register all their guns previous to the shoot.~~

(4) 3   The registration of Trench Mortars will begin at 4 p.m.

(5) 4   Officers Commanding Batteries concerned, or their represent-
atives, will meet the Trench Mortar Officer at Point N.14.1,
where RIFLEMAN AVENUE enters front line, at 3 p.m.

(6) 5   Batteries concerned will arrange telephonic and visual
communication from front line to their O. s.

                                                    Lieut., R. F. A.
                                          Adjutant Left Group R. F. A.

        Time ....

Copy No. 1   filed.
         2   R.A., 38th Div.
         3   114th Inf. Bde.
         4   "A"/121.
         5   "C"/121.
         6   Lieut., W.J.Jones.
         7   War Diary.
         8

SECRET.   COPY NO...... 9

OPERATION ORDER NO 7. BY LIEUT., COL., P.J. PATERSON D.S.O,

R.F.A. COMMANDING LEFT GROUP R.F.A. 38th D.A. (W.A.C.).

Headquarters   Saturday   3rd June 1916.

Map Reference Sheet 36 S.W.1.

(1) Intention.- That 25 men of the 14th will raid the enemy's trenches at N.19.a.3.0. at about 11 pm. 4.6.1916. At this hour the raiding party will be lining the ditch in NO MAN'S LAND from N.19.a.1.6½. to N.19.a.2.8. Other raids are to be carried out at the same time near WICK and BIRD CAGE.

(2) The following Batteries will fire as under.-

"A"/122:- one sec. firing from M.21.b.8.6½. on M.G. emplacement near the salient at N.19.a.3.5. This section will be moved to the new position on the night of 3.6.1916. and registered on the morning of 4.6.1916. This sec. will open fire at 11 pm. and will fire intense fire for two minutes, after which it will lift 50 yards for 30 secs, then another 50 yards for 30 secs, then another 50 yards for 30 secs, and so on until the total lift is 300 yards. After 2 mins. and 30 secs. the rate of fire will be gradually reduced until the rate of fire is 2 rounds per gun per minute. Total time from commence to cease fire 20 minutes.
One sec :- This sec. will open fire at 11 pm. and fire intense fire for 20 minutes, from N.19.a.3.2.to N.19.c.2.8.
"B"/119. one gun. will fire slow fire all the time from 11 to 11.40 pm from N.19.a.8.5. to N.19.b.2.0.
"B"/119. one gun. - will fire from N.19.c.4.2. to N.19.c.4.8½.
          one sec. - will fire from N.19.a.6.8. to N.19.c.7½.1.
These three guns will fire intense fire from 11.20 pm to 11.40 pm
"D"/122. one sec:- on N.19.a.8½.5.
          one sec:- WICK Salient N.19.d.2.6.
"D"/122 will fire at a medium rate of fire from 11.20 pm to 11.40 pm.

(3) Captain Williams will be in direct command of two 18-pdr Batteries, and the Howitzer Battery.

(4) Captain Williams will arrange for the necessary telephonic and visual communication to such a point in the front trenches as indicated by Lieut., Col., Hayes Commanding 14th Welsh. Captain Williams will arrange for the F.O.O. to work in conjunction with the Infantry Commander - Lieut., Col, Hayes. Watches will be synchronized at Left Group Headquarters at 6 pm. 4.6.1916. All Battery Commanders must have their watches synchronized.

(5) Captain Williams will be at C.R.As. House at 10 pm on the 4.6.1916.

Copy.No 1 filed.
     " 2 R.A.38th Div.
     " 3 114th Inf.Bde.
     " 4 Lt.Col.Hayes.
     " 5 Rt Group.
     " 6 "A"/122.
     " 7 "B"/119.
     " 8 "D"/122
     " 9 War Diary
     " 10

                                              Lieut R.F.A.
                                     Adjutant 119th Brigade R.F.A.

SECRET. Copy No. 18

OPERATION ORDER NO. 6, BY LIEUT., COL., P.J.PATERSON D.S.O.,
R.F.A., COMMANDING LEFT GROUP R.F.A., 38th D.A., (W. A. C.)

Headquarters   Saturday   3rd June 1916.

Map reference.- Sheet 36 S.W.1.

(1) Intention.- That 50 men of the 10th Welsh will raid the enemy's trenches at about N.14.a.8.4. at 11 pm. 4.6.1916. At this hour the raiding party will be lining the ditch in NO MANS LAND from N.14.a.4½.6 to N.14.a.6.4. Other raids are to be carried out at the same time near TRIVELET and the BIRD CAGE

(2) The following Batteries will fire as under for two minutes - Starting at 11 pm., and firing at the rate of 5 rounds per gun per minute.
"C"/121, the enfilade Battery, will fire on the point of assault at N.14.a.8.4.
"A"/119 will fire from N.14.a.9½.5. to N.14.b.2½.9.
"A"/121 will fire from N.14.c.4½.9½ to N.13.d.9.8.
These three Batteries will be under the direct Command of Captain Pryce.
"D"/120 Howitzer Battery, will fire.- one section on the SUGAR LOAF-N.8.d.5½.1.; one section on the WICK SALIENT - N.13.d.3.8. to N.13.d.5.7½.
At 11.2pm. "C"/121 will switch its fire to the left on to the German Support Line for 30 secs, after which it will again switch another 100 yards to the left, when the rate of fire will be gradually reduced to two rounds per gun per minute. This barrage will be kept up for 15 minutes. Enfilade Battery will fire T. shrapnel only.
At 11.2 pm "A"/119 and "A"/121 will gradually drop their rate of fire to 2 rounds per gun per minute.

Rate of fire of "D"/120, 3 rounds per gun per minute until 11.2 pm. when rate of fire will be gradually reduced to 1 round per gun per minute.

(3) Captain Pryce will arrange the necessary telephonic and visual communication to such a point in the front trenches as indicated by Col., Ricketts.
Captain Pryce will arrange for the F.O.O. to work in conjunction with Infantry Commander, Col., Ricketts, at N.14.a.3½.7½.
Watches will be synchronized at Group Headquarters at 6 pm., 4.6.1916.
All Battery Commanders must have their watches synchronized.

(4) Captain Pryce will be at the BRISTOL O.P. at 10.30 pm. 4.6.1916.

Time.......

Copy No 1 filed
     2 R.A.38th Div.
     3 114 Inf Bde.
     4 Col. Ricketts.
     5 "A"/119.
     6 "A"/121.
     7 "C"/121.
     8 "D"/120.
     9 Rt Group.
    10 War Diary.
    11

Lieut R.F.A.
Adjutant Left Group R.F.A.

CONFIDENTIAL.

WAR DIARY.

119th Brigade
R.F.A.

Month of
May
1916

SECRET.   Copy No......9......

OPERATION ORDER NO. 4, BY LIEUT., COL., P.J.PATERSON D.S.O., R.F.A.,
COMMANDING LEFT GROUP R.F.A., 38th DIVISIONAL ARTILLERY, (W.A.C.).

Headquarters   Monday   29th May 1916.

Map reference Sheet 36.S.W. 1, Edition 6.

1. Intention is to breach front and support parapet and wire at N.13.d.5.7., by Trench Mortars, on 31.5.1916.

2. "A" 121 - 18 pdr. Battery)
   "B" 119 - 18 pdr. Battery)
   "D" 120 - How. Battery   ) will co-operate in covering the registration of Trench Mortars, and complete the breach after the Trench Mortars have completed their shoot, should the latter not succeed in making a breach. During the time the Trench Mortars are registering, "A" 121 and "B" 119 will engage the enemy's parapet on the respective flanks of the proposed breach to keep the enemy's heads down.

3. The 18 pdr. Batteries will register all their guns previous to the shoot, and should they be called upon to make a breach, will fire rounds of Battery fire - 15 secs. The shooting to be carried out in batches of 20 rounds per Battery by each 18 pdr. Battery in rotation, commencing with the right Battery - "B" 119 - first.

4. The Howitzer Battery, if called upon to breach, will do so deliberately and independently of the 18pdr. Batteries.

5. The registration of Trench Mortars will begin at 4 pm.

6. Officers Commanding Batteries concerned, will meet Lieut., O.J.Jones or his representative, at the FARM O.P., at 3.15 pm., 31.5.1916.

7. All Batteries concerned will arrange telephonic and visual communication from front line trench to FARM O.P.

8. The Group Commander will be at the FARM O.P., at 3.15pm.

                                                W.D.Cook Lieut., R. F. A.
                                                Adjutant Left Group R. F. A.

Copy No. 1 filed.
      " 2 R.A., 38th Divn.
      " 3 114th Inf. Bde.
      " 4 "A" 121.
      " 5 "B" 119.
      " 6 "D" 120.
      " 7 Lieut., O.J.Jones.
      " 8 War Diary.
      " 9

38th Div.
XV.Corps.

Division transferred
from II.Corps, Fourth
Army, 3.7.16.

WAR DIARY

Headquarters,

119th BRIGADE, R.F.A.

J U L Y'

1 9 1 6

Attached:

War Diary of "A" Battery,
20/29.7.16.
War Diary of "B" Battery,
20/25.7.16.
War Diary of "C" Battery,
20/31.7.16.

119th Brigade.
R.F.A.

WAR DIARY
or
INTELLIGENCE SUMMARY.

Army Form C. 2118.

Maps Ref. LENS 11
" AMIENS 17.
" " FRANCE 62 A N.E.
" FRANCE 62 A N.E.

38 Army

Place	Date	Hour	Summary of Events and Information	Remarks and references to Appendices
MIRVAUX	1.7.16		"B" & "C" & "D" Btys arrived at 2.15 a.m. "A" & "B" Btys reported from detachment at 4.30 a.m. The whole Brigade received orders at 9 p.m. to move off at 11.30 p.m. for HARPONVILLE. Moved off at that hour and continued march.	Wrote
HARPONVILLE	2.7.16.		Arrived at this place at 2.30 a.m.	Wrote
"	3.7.16.		Rested during day. Orders received to march to TREUX WOOD at 11 p.m.	Wrote
TREUX WOOD	4.7.16		Arrived in bivouac at 5.30 a.m. C.O. & a complement of Officers reconnoitered gun positions towards front line near MONTAUBAN, with a view to taking over positions in line.	Wrote
"	5.7.16		Reconnaissance by Officers of new positions continued.	Wrote
"	6.7.16		Reconnaissance by Officers. Nothing to Report.	Wrote
"	7.7.16			Wrote
"	8.7.16		Orders received of "Probable move to action tonight". "A" & "B" & "D" Btys & B.H.Q. moved forward coming into action in Bois d'antique in F.8.b. and F.9.a. sheet France 62 A N.E. B.H.Q. located at F.8.a.6.3. just - S. West of FRICOURT.	Wrote

WAR DIARY or INTELLIGENCE SUMMARY

Army Form C. 2118.

Map: FRANCE 62 d NE / 57 D S.E. / 57 C S.W.

Place	Date	Hour	Summary of Events and Information	Remarks and references to Appendices
FRICOURT	9.7.16		Btys. in Action all day registering portions of MAMETZ WOOD & BNTALMAISON and Vicinity, no casualties	WATR
"	10.7.16		Continued in Action until evening. "C" Bty moved up from wagon line at TREUX WOOD to wagon line at E 12 a 3.3. "A" & "B" Btys moved to wire cutting positions at X 22 c. "D" Bty remain in Action in F 8 c.	WATR
"	11.7.16		"A" & "B" Btys registered enemy wire at second line in front of BAZENTIN LE PETIT WOOD. "A" Bty had one man killed and "B" Bty one man wounded. "C" Bty moved from wagon line to Action alongside other two Btys in X 22 c.	WATR
"	12.7.16		Wire cutting by all three Btys continued. "D" Bty continuous deliberate bombardment of Enemys second line. "C" Bty one man killed and three wounded by shell fire about 9 am. "A" Bty 3 men killed and four wounded.	WATR
"	13.7.16		Wire cutting continued by all Batteries and registering Bombardment of enemy's front and support lines carried out. 2nd Lt Sapster wounded.	WATR
"	14.7.16		Bombardment of enemy's villages and woods in conjunction with Infy. attack from 3.30 am to 6.50 am. Attack successful. "D" Bty two men killed one wounded. 2 Lt. M. P. Fitzgerald killed	WATR

WAR DIARY or INTELLIGENCE SUMMARY

Army Form C. 2118

Map Ref. FRANCE 57D.S.E.
" " " 57C.S.E.
" " " 57C.S.W.
" " " 57 D.

Place	Date	Hour	Summary of Events and Information	Remarks and references to Appendices
FRICOURT	14.7.16		2 Lt. P.J. Conner wounded. Btys fired on various objectives throughout whole day and night.	WDR
"	15.7.16.		D Bty having got out of range during the steady advance, moved forward to a new posn in X.24.c. Btys. engaged all day in supporting various small infantry attacks.	WDR
"	16.7.16		Orders received to fire bursts of fire on MARTINPUICH (M32) throughout day + night.	WDR
"	17.7.16.		B H.Q. moved to X.22.c. old German dug outs in front of SHELTER WOOD. Shelling continued same as on previous day.	WDR
"	18.7.16		Position shelled during the night - and early morning with "tear" shells. 'C' Bty. had five casualties (wounded). Orders received to vacate position by 12 midnight + Rendezvous at TREUX WOOD.	WDR
"	19.7.16		Brigade in rendezvous at TREUX WOOD by 4 a.m. Marched at 4.30 p.m. by road to ST. LEGER.	WDR
ST. LEGER	20.7.16		Arrived at St. LEGER at 1.30 a.m. A.B. + C Btys went into action at K27a.1.1. relieving A.B. + C Btys 2nd + 3rd Brigade in action at K27a.1.1. Bde H.Qrs. ST. LEGER. K27C.2.7. and K20 C.5.5. respectively. D Bty in wagon line at same place.	WDR

WAR DIARY
or
INTELLIGENCE SUMMARY

(Erase heading not required.)

Army Form C. 2118

Map ref. FRANCE 57 D.

Place	Date	Hour	Summary of Events and Information	Remarks and references to Appendices
ST LEGER	21.7.16 to 24.7.16		Nothing to report.	WDC
MAILLY	25.7.16		Lt. Col. P.J. Paterson Comdg 119th Brigade took over command of a new Group R.F.A. called "Regier Group" consisting of Bties. A/120 D/119 and C/122. All moved into action D/119 located at — Q1.d.1.4. Both Hqrs. at — P.6.a.5.3. Taken over by 6 p.m.	WDC
MAILLY	26.7.16		Personnel of A/120 relieved by personnel of B/119 in action at K.31.c.6.3. Final consisting at relieved point at night.	WDC
MAILLY	27.7.16 to 29.7.16		Nothing special to report.	WDC
MAILLY	30.7.16		2 Lt. M.P. Fitzgerald previously reported wounded on 14th rejoined the Brigade from Hosp. and re-posted to his Bty C.	WDC
MAILLY	31.7.16		Nothing to report	WDC

OM Paterson
Lt. Col. R.F.A.
Comdg 119 Bde R.F.A.
31.7.16.

WAR DIARY "A" Bty 119th Brigade R.F.A.
or
INTELLIGENCE SUMMARY

Army Form C. 2118

Place	Date	Hour	Summary of Events and Information	Remarks and references to Appendices
In front of SERRE	9/7/16		Took over Battery position from B/343. Gone covering northern half of SERRE to beginning of PUISIEUX-AU-MONT. woods. Group Commander Lt. Col. Head. 120th Brigade R.F.A. Covering 23rd Battalion. Right Brigade.	
	24/7/16		Lieut Bt. Clark went to School of Instruction. Heavy French howitzer Beaune Contre Group in place of Right Group. Covering 24th Battalion of Centre Brigade.	
	29/7/16		20th Division Infantry took over from 38th Division.	

Capt.
O.C. A/119 R.F.A.
31/7/16

WAR DIARY of 13/19 Bth R.F.A.
or
INTELLIGENCE SUMMARY

Army Form C. 2118

Place	Date	Hour	Summary of Events and Information	Remarks and references to Appendices
COUIN	20.7.16	6pm	Battery from bivouac at J7a8.6 relieved Battery of 48th Divn, K27a2.7. Relief completed at 6pm. Battery covering front from K29 central to K29b6.6. O.P at M33B3.6 – Waggon line in bivouac as above.	Apps
	21/7/16	10am 5.30pm	Carried out registration on zone as above. Cut wire at K29 B2.1. Some damage done. Shelled support line in June at night. Ammn expended 137 rounds – this is daily allotment until further mentioned in diary	Apps Apps
	22nd	12noon to 3pm	Fired in support Sur in Jordan	Apps
	23rd		Shelled Sap and Wire at K29B10 – Carried out registration Shelled sap at K28B10 & front line K 29 B9.5	Apps Apps
	24th		Shelled support line in K29B. Changed Comparator to K30C7.3. Exchanging with A/120. Relief completed 6pm. Came under orders of Right Group 38th Div. (114th Bty R.F.A.)	Apps

Army Form C. 2118

Instructions regarding War Diaries and Intelligence Summaries are contained in F.S. Regs., Part II. and the Staff Manual respectively. Title Pages will be prepared in manuscript.

C/119 Bde. RFA WAR DIARY or INTELLIGENCE SUMMARY

(Erase heading not required.)

Place	Date	Hour	Summary of Events and Information	Remarks and references to Appendices
COLINCAMPS Wagon Lines at ST. LEGER	20 Feb 1916		Attached to Right Group (266. HEAD) and relieved C/243 (48th Div.) in action at K.20.c.4.3. Guns taken over; one handed over to 125 D.A. All prepared positions for guns now lined in old British bdqrs. dug-outs 100 yards distant. O.P. in old support trench in K.21 central. Zone K.29 central to K.23.9.6. A/119 & B/119 also divided the same zone (11°52'&11°54') C/119 chiefly employed in support trenches.	
	21.		Shelled SERRE – PUISIEUX road and fire trenches in K.29.6 SW during night: about 50 rounds. Registration. Night firing on SERRE – PUISIEUX road and support trenches in K.29.6. Water party pit. Some 10″ shells 150 yards from battery. 2 guns bellows up started 100 rounds	
	22.		G.O.C. 28th Div. visited position. Dull day. Found officer of Battn. Hdqrs. (every third night). Shelled transport on SERRE – PUISIEUX road 1.30 am. One party gun infantry, and trench road during the night. Fired about 120 rounds in all.	LEAKSONES attle from B/119
	23		Registration continued. Little Rifle fire in trenches; some near RED COTTAGE (K.28.a.) C gun at action with return fire to ammunition wagon. Usual night firing. About 130 rounds in all.	
	24.		Port light till 5 pm. Retaliated on three occasions for T.M. fire on front trenches. Dull pile. registration on night of zone, & also two points on SERRE road. Shelled party on southwick K.25.a N.W. Night firing on SERRE PUISIEUX road., ammunition railway S.W. for SERRE, & trench junction in K.30.a 9 to 10 pm & 12 to 1 am. Fired 134 rounds. R2. material obtained from fig. fil.	
	25.		Construction of gun pits proceeded with. Dull day with light intervals. Reported on Rift group fast. Night firing as usual. Ammunition allowance increased to 220 rounds per day.	
	26.		Construction of new Right Group (A.B.C.D/120, A.C/119). Zone as before. Also upkeeping O/M. on formation	

1875. Wt. W593/826 1,000,000 4/15 J.B.C. & A. A.D.S.S./Forms/C. 2118.

Army Form C. 2118

WAR DIARY
INTELLIGENCE SUMMARY
(Erase heading not required.)

Place	Date	Hour	Summary of Events and Information	Remarks and references to Appendices
COLINCAMPS	26.		Dull day; Lit light after 6 p.m. Ships Bombarded front line & wire in right of zone observed from Battn. Hdqrs. Much night firing.	
	27.		Heat wave commenced. Foggy morning. Very bright afternoon. German aeroplanes more active.	
	28th		Much hostile T.M. activity. Retaliated throughout afternoon.	
	29.		38th Div. Inf. relieved by 20th. C/119 covers Oxford & Bucks L.I. Battn. of 60th Bde. German Saxonian Ballons up all afternoon. English aeroplane bombs Battery near NW. edge of SERRE wood; some movement seen; and Engaged dugout K.25.a.1.8. in Rd evening.	Lt. M.R. FITZGERALD rejoined from hospital.
	30.		Very fit day. Foggy till 10 a.m. Shelled Rd orchard K 25.a. 1.8. in Rd evening SERRE in Place where 2 Germans seen running. Night firing as usual; PUISIEUX, Battn. H.Qrs and Trench Mortar emplacements engaged.	
	31.		Hotter still. Trench Mortar located and bombarded; 100 yards west of SERRE wood. Storage in SERRE (K.30.a.9.1) engaged.	

[signature] Capt RHA
Cmdg 119 Bde. RFA

119th Brigade R.F.A. Ty.

Army Form C. 2118.
MAP. Ref. FRANCE S 7 D. 1/40,000

Vol 9

WAR DIARY
or
INTELLIGENCE SUMMARY.
(Erase heading not required.)

Instructions regarding War Diaries and Intelligence Summaries are contained in F.S. Regs., Part II. and the Staff Manual respectively. Title pages will be prepared in manuscript.

Hour, Date, Place	Summary of Events and Information	Remarks and references to Appendices
MAILLY MAILLET. 1.8.16 to 3.8.16	Nothing to report. Wire cutting and retaliation carried out.	W.D.C.
" 4.8.16	A smoke barrage scheme was organized, but owing to wind only the artillery part of the bombardment was carried out. B/119 fired about 100 and 150 rounds from 9.03 p.m. to 9.06 p.m. & 9.10 p.m. to 9.13 p.m. respectively. D/119 fired about 30 and 70 rounds at the same times at Redan & Tenries Junction. Little retaliation.	W.D.C.
" 5.8.16	Orders received that the Group will be relieved in action by various units, on 6/7 on 7/8 and 8/9.	W.D.C.
" 6.8.16	One section each of A/119 & C/119 relieved in action by B/161 & C/161 respectively.	W.D.C.
" 7.8.16	Remaining sections of A/119 & C/119 relieved. One section of B/119 & D/119 relieved by 111 TRBy & 43rd Bty respectively.	W.D.C.

WAR DIARY
or
INTELLIGENCE SUMMARY.

(Erase heading not required.)

MAP. Ref. FRANCE 57D. 1/40,000.
" " HAZEBROUCK Army Form C. 2118.

Hour, Date, Place	Summary of Events and Information	Remarks and references to Appendices
MAILLY-MAILLET. 8.8.16	All Bty. Wagon lines moved to THIEVRES. Remaining sections of B/119 & D/119 relieved and B.H.Q. Wagon lines also moved to THIEVRES. Command of Right-trench handed over by Lt-Col. P.J. Patterson to Lt. Col. Forsyth at 3 P.M. 3 8th Bgn. 1 Dvn. and reported B.H.Q.	WDC
THIEVRES 9.8.16	Arrived at 1 a.m. All Btys being in billets at the same place. Received orders to march at 7 a.m. tomorrow.	WDC
HEM 10.8.16	Arrived in Bivouac at HEM at 9 a.m. B Hqrs located at A11 d 8.5.	WDC
" 11.8.16	Rested	WDC
" 12.8.16	Orders received to entrain and move from 3rd Army Area to 2nd Army Area at ESQUELBECQ on 13.8.16	WDC
ZEGGERS-CAPPEL 13.8.16	All Btys moved by train at different hours commencing with A/119 at 4.34 P.M. arriving in billets about 11 P.M. B/119 arrived at 2 P.M. with B/119. C & D Btys arrived at three hours intervals, D arriving about 5 P.M. B Hqrs in ZEGGERS-CAPPEL just E. of the Church.	WDC

WAR DIARY or INTELLIGENCE SUMMARY.

MAP REF. BELGIUM & *France* Army Form C.2118.
FRANCE Sheet 27 - 1/40,000
BELGIUM 28N.W. 1/20,000

Hour, Date, Place	Summary of Events and Information	Remarks and references to Appendices
ZEGGERS-CAPPEL 14.8.16 to 18.8.16	Nothing to report. Whole Brigade in rest. Usual exercises for horses and men and equipment being refitted &c.	WDC
" " 19.8.16	Bde Sports held to-day very successful. The C.O. Brigade went forward to reconnoitre positions in new area N of YPRES.	WDC
" " 20.8.16	C.O. and Bty Comdrs with four signallers each went forward to new area to begin taking over.	WDC
TROIS-TOUR 21.8.16	A, C, & D Btys relieved one section each of 125, 126 & 128 Btys respectively. One section of B Bty also relieved one section of D.E. H/119 for tactical purposes. D 125 Bty and comes under command of Lt. Col. Paterson assumed command of the Left Group 38 Division from 8 a.m. to-day.	WDC
" 22.8.16	Btys see completed relief at 12 midnight	WDC

Map Ref. Sheet 28 NW 1/20000

Army Form C. 2118.

WAR DIARY
or
INTELLIGENCE SUMMARY.
(Erase heading not required.)

Instructions regarding War Diaries and Intelligence Summaries are contained in F. S. Regs., Part II. and the Staff Manual respectively. Title pages will be prepared in manuscript.

Hour, Date, Place	Summary of Events and Information	Remarks and references to Appendices
TROIS-TOURS. 23.8.16	Extremely quiet. Btys carried out registration in new positions. All Btys are in action as follows A/119. 4 guns at B2d.1.8 2 guns at B2a.9.9½.B/119. 4 guns at B28.6.83 D/119. 2 guns at B32.0.9½.5 and 2 guns at B2a.2.3. Brigade Hdqrs at TROIS-TOURS. B2.8 at 7.2.	WJC
" 24.8.16 to 26.8.16	Very quiet days. Nothing occurred of interest, usual registration and Hostile shelling latter very scattered and non-effective.	WJC
" 27.8.16	Orders received re-reorganisation of the Artillery to take effect almost immediately	WJC
" 28.8.16	C Bty 119 sent one section each to A & B Btys making them both six guns. 18 pdr Bty.	WJC

Forms/C. 2118/10

WAR DIARY

INTELLIGENCE SUMMARY.

(Erase heading not required.)

Map ref Sheet 28 NW/1.50000   Army Form C. 2118.

Hour, Date, Place	Summary of Events and Information	Remarks and references to Appendices
TROIS-TOURS 29.8.16	A. & B. Btys. are commanded by Capt. C. Payne & E.A. Wood respectively. D.120 Bty. 4.5" Army joined the Brigade becoming C/119 Bty. The Brigade now consists of A Bty. 18 pdr Capt C. Payne. B Bty 18 pdr 6 guns Capt E.A Wood's C Bty. 4.5" How. four guns Capt W.M. Matheson. D Bty. 4.5" How. four guns Capt P. Wyse.	WDC
" 30.8.16	Very little firing on either side. Weather conditions bad	WDC
" 31.8.16	Very quiet day	WDC

Wallace

Lt Col R.F.A.

Comdg. 119th Brigade R.F.A.

31.8.16

Army Form C. 2118

WAR DIARY
or
INTELLIGENCE SUMMARY
(Erase heading not required.)

Instructions regarding War Diaries and Intelligence Summaries are contained in F. S. Regs., Part II. and the Staff Manual respectively. Title Pages will be prepared in manuscript.

Place	Date	Hour	Summary of Events and Information	Remarks and references to Appendices
			CONFIDENTIAL WAR DIARY OF C Battery 119th Brigade R.F.A from 1st August 1916 to 9th August 1916	

SECRET

WAR DIARY
119th Brigade.
R.F.A

Month of
August 1916

WAR DIARY
or
INTELLIGENCE SUMMARY.

(Erase heading not required.)

A/119.R.F.A

Army Form C. 2118.

Place	Date	Hour	Summary of Events and Information	Remarks and references to Appendices
K 21 a.1.1. Sheet 57D Battery Position	1/8/16		Battery in action opposite SERRE - under Lieut-Col C.O.HEAD (120th Bde R.F.A.) Group Commander Capt. C.a.R.PRYCE - admitted to Hospital - Lieut R.GRESLEY assumed temporary command of Battery.	
	2/8/16		Lieut D. LONERAGAN attached to Battery, from C/119.R.F.A. Battery was shelled with 15.0 & 10.5 cm. No casualties - no material damage.	
	3/8/16		Major ARCHDALE O.C. B/61. R.F.A. 20th Division visited Battery, with view to relieving same in the Line. Battery attached 20th Division. Battery shelled lightly	
	4/8/16		Battery commenced cutting wire at selected spot in front of SERRE. 3 Gunners & 2 Drivers bolted to Battery to complete Establishment	
	5/8/16		About 200 rds. 10.5cm. 15cm & 77cm fell in & around Battery during day Capt. C.a.R PRYCE returned from Hospital & re-assumed command of Battery Lieut. R.GRESLEY wounded in head by shell splinter at Battery Position admitted to Hospital	
	6/8/16		Battery continued cutting wire in front of SERRE Battery continued cutting wire. Right Section relieved by section of B/61 R.F.A. returned to wagon Lines. Major ARCHDALE arrived & was installed in post.	
	7/8/16		Relief of Battery by B/61 R.F.A. completed & Battery assembled at wagon lines - J.7 a 3 & 4 Sheet 57D. Major ARCHDALE took over command of Battery Position	
	8/8/16		Battery marched to THIÈVRES (T.1 d 9.7.) rejoined E/119.R Brigade. 38th (welsh) Division	

C.a.R Pryce Capt
O.C. A/119 R.F.A.

Army Form C. 2118

WAR DIARY
or
INTELLIGENCE SUMMARY
(Erase heading not required.)

Instructions regarding War Diaries and Intelligence Summaries are contained in F.S. Regs., Part II. and the Staff Manual respectively. Title Pages will be prepared in manuscript.

Place	Date August	Hour	Summary of Events and Information	Remarks and references to Appendices
CALLISCAMPS (2nd Ref) 20 Div 2/F	1st		Wire cutting & bombardment by left gun (on left).	
	2		Very Lt. Forward O.P. selected in SANSON Trench Guinecourt. T.M. activity on our front.	
	3		Wire cutting 250 rounds. Maj. TOPPIN (9/61 Grah. Arty.) visited O.P.	
	4		Group Commander (Capt. Guy. 111th Head) & Lt. Col. BRYANT (61st Bde) visited O.P. Also officer from Ammunition allowance 450 rounds per diem. C/61. Wire cutting 300 rounds.	"LT. A.B. PASMORE joining C/119 from England
	5		Colder & very clear. E winds. Many pillars up. Wire cutting at Pt. 2 from K 29 t 69	
	6		[HERUTERNE map] 250 rounds. Much aeroplane & balloon activity. Valley ground 400 x left of Btry. heavily shelled. Wire cutting 360 rounds. at R 29 t 50. 1 German seen to be killed. A/119 shelled.	
ST LEGER	7		Left Acc. (Lt. M.K. JONES) reloaded By Sec. of 6/61. 9.30 pm. & marched to wagon line. (ST. LEGER) all shells near A City. Wire cutting 300 rounds. Ammo allotted with 4.7mm on Flanders 9.30 pm until completed after which was line	
THIEVRES	8		Restful day. delightful weather. Marched 5 am. to THIEVRES (3 miles).	
	9		Good billets. Refitcars now being attached. Very put all Btys in 111th Bde. together again. Gas guard in afternoon.	

J.R.H. Capt. R.F.A.
O.C. C/119 Bde R.F.A.

119th Brigade R.F.A. **WAR DIARY** Map Reference Sheet Army Form C. 2118. 28 BELGIUM 1/40000

INTELLIGENCE SUMMARY.

(Erase heading not required.)

Hour, Date, Place	Summary of Events and Information	Remarks and references to Appendices
TROIS TOURS 1.9.16 to 5.9.16	Nothing occured except the usual shelling and retaliation on both sides.	WDC
" " 6.9.16	Enemy slightly more active	WDC
" " 7.9.16 to 9.9.16	Nothing to report	WDC
" " 10.9.16	Scheme for wire cutting and bombardment arranged. Copy attached — Sections of A/119 & B/119 in place for scheme.	WDC
" " 11.9.16 to 13.9.16	Nothing to report	WDC
" " 14.9.16	We carried out a pre-arranged Bombardment of the Enemy front line and support trench, in accordance with a pre-arrangement. It was apparently very successful from C.13.d.8.8 to C.14.c.7.5.9.3.	WDC

WAR DIARY or INTELLIGENCE SUMMARY

Army Form C. 2118

Map Ref. Belgium Sheet 28 1/40,000

Place	Date	Hour	Summary of Events and Information	Remarks and references to Appendices
TROISTOURS	14.9.16		Enemy scarcely any retaliation	W.D.C
"	15.9.16		Wire cutting carried out in the morning on the same place as yesterday, from 11.15 p.m. to 12 m.d. Heavy Bombardment of Enemy front line and support trenches from C.13.b.8.8 to C.14.c.7.5. 9.5. Also hurts of fire at same place throughout remainder of night - Very little retaliation -	W.D.C
"	16.9.16		Quiet day	W.D.C
"	17.9.16		Began wire cutting with A/119 and B/119 Bty on a front at C.14.a.3½.2 to clear space for a raid - small gap cut -	W.D.C
"	18.9.16		Almost incessant & short. Heavy rain had light - Operation Orders completed for said. Copy attached.	W.D.C
"	19.9.16		A/119 & B/119 Cut wire at same place and extended gap - to clear space for raiders to pass through	W.D.C
"	20.9.16		A, B & D/119 Bombarded selected points from 2 a.m. to about 2.15 a.m. when they were stopped as the raid did not come off	W.D.C

WAR DIARY
or
INTELLIGENCE SUMMARY

Army Form C. 2118

Map Ref. Sheet 28. 1/40,000
" " 27. 1/40,000

Place	Date	Hour	Summary of Events and Information	Remarks and references to Appendices
TROISTOURS	21.9.16		Lt Col Pringle took over Group Hqrs relieving Lt Col Patterson	W.D.C
"	22.9.16		Both Hqrs moved to PROVEN (SHEET 27) leaving Hqs in action	W.D.C
PROVEN	23.9.16 to 28.9.16		Nothing to report.	W.D.C
REGERSBURG	29.9.16		Bde. Hqrs moved up to take over Right Group Hqrs relieving 122 Bde Hqrs.	W.D.C
"	"		Relief completed. Only one Bty of 119 Brigade in Group i.e. C/119. Group consists of all Btys 122 Brigade in addition and C/121 Brigade.	W.D.C

Signed
Lt Col R.F.A.
Comdg 119th Brigade R.F.A.
30.9.16

Army Form C. 2118

WAR DIARY
or
INTELLIGENCE SUMMARY

(Erase heading not required.)

Instructions regarding War Diaries and Intelligence Summaries are contained in F. S. Regs., Part II. and the Staff Manual respectively. Title Pages will be prepared in manuscript.

Place	Date	Hour	Summary of Events and Information	Remarks and references to Appendices

1875 Wt. W593/826 1,000,000 4/15 J.B.C. & A. A.D.S.S./Forms/C. 2118.

Army Form C. 2118

WAR DIARY
or
INTELLIGENCE SUMMARY

(Erase heading not required.)

Instructions regarding War Diaries and Intelligence Summaries are contained in F. S. Regs., Part II. and the Staff Manual respectively. Title Pages will be prepared in manuscript.

Place	Date	Hour	Summary of Events and Information	Remarks and references to Appendices

1875 Wt. W593/826 1,000,000 4/15 J.B.C. & A. A.D.S.S./Forms/C. 2118.

Army Form C. 2118

WAR DIARY
or
INTELLIGENCE SUMMARY

of B/119 BDE RFA

(Erase heading not required.)

Instructions regarding War Diaries and Intelligence Summaries are contained in F.S. Regs., Part II. and the Staff Manual respectively. Title Pages will be prepared in manuscript.

Place	Date	Hour	Summary of Events and Information	Remarks and references to Appendices
BRIELEN FM. B26 B8.6.	23/8/16	4.25 pm	Fired 75 rounds to cut wire at C14 a 4.2 - successful in widening existing gap. Hostile artillery very quiet.	Ref. 28 NW ST JULIEN 1/10000 Ed 3D Eaw
	24th		Fired 4 rounds at M.G. emplacement C14 a 7.0	Eaw
	25th		Fired at an aeroplane	Eaw
	26th	3 pm	Carried out registration of points C7 B 2.6 (trench junction) C2 C 6.7 (roads) C7 d 8.6, C8 C 0.1 (front line) which enfilade X-rd at C26 C 4.1½ -	
		5.30 pm	Fired 6 rounds on T.M'y retaliation at trench junction C14 a 25.70 at request of 13th R.W.F.	Eaw
	27th	7.15 pm	" 33 " "	Eaw
		7 pm	" 22 " "	Eaw

Army Form C. 2118

WAR DIARY of B/119 Bde R.F.A.
or INTELLIGENCE SUMMARY
(Erase heading not required.)

Place	Date	Hour	Summary of Events and Information	Remarks and references to Appendices
BRIELEN FM B28A6.6	28/9/16	4:30 pm	Fired 78 rounds to reopen gap in wire at C14a 4.2 — Effect poor owing to irregular fuzes	Eaw
		11:30 pm	Bombardment in support of raid by 13th R.W.F. on C14a 4.2 — 11:30pm – 11:32pm 4 guns on C14a 3¾.4 – C14a 3½.2½ – C14a 3½.4 (communication trench) 2 guns at fire 5 secs – C14a 6.2½ – C14a 53¾ Pause 11:32pm – 11:34pm — 11:34pm – 11:36pm As above repeated 11:36 pm raising fuzy entered enemy trench under 11:36 – 11:56pm Barrage 4 guns C14a 3½.4 – C14a 4.5½ 2 guns C14a 6.4 2½ – C14a 53¾ at X fire 10 secs 16 x 2 fire 30 secs 11:56 slowed down to x fire raiders party returned 17 men obtained firing	

Army Form C. 2118

WAR DIARY
or
INTELLIGENCE SUMMARY

(Erase heading not required.)

Instructions regarding War Diaries and Intelligence Summaries are contained in F.S. Regs., Part II. and the Staff Manual respectively. Title Pages will be prepared in manuscript.

Place	Date	Hour	Summary of Events and Information	Remarks and references to Appendices
BRIELEN FM B28B86	29th 9/16	—	Nil —	Ems
	30th	4 am	4 am fired 42 rounds at trench junction C14a7.0 — in retaliation for TM fire at request of 14th R.W.F.	Ems

30/9/16

[signatures] Capt RFA
B/81 Bde RFA

Army Form C. 2118

WAR DIARY
or
INTELLIGENCE SUMMARY

A/119. R.F.A.

(Erase heading not required.)

Place	Date	Hour	Summary of Events and Information	Remarks and references to Appendices
B.22.d.1-8	23/9/16		Battery came under command of Lt Col. Pringle on his assuming command of Left Group. R.F.A.	C.P.
DAWSON'S CORNER Sheet	26/9/16		Moved Right Section forward to position at C.25.d. 5.9. on east side of Canal. for purpose of covering raid.	C.P.
ST JULIEN 1/10000	28/9/16		Battery in action covering raiding party of 13th R.W.F. on C14a 4½.2. from 11.30pm to 12 midnight	C.P.
	29/9/16		Brought back Right Section from forward position.	C.P.

C.P. Catt
Comdg. A/119 R.F.A.

Army Form C. 2118.

WAR DIARY
or
INTELLIGENCE SUMMARY.
(Erase heading not required.)

Week ending 30/9/16 D/119/RFA.

Instructions regarding War Diaries and Intelligence Summaries are contained in F.S. Regs., Part II. and the Staff Manual respectively. Title pages will be prepared in manuscript.

Place	Date	Hour	Summary of Events and Information	Remarks and references to Appendices
In the Field BRIELEN.	23/Sept/16		Lt. J.O. Williams went on leave	
"	24		Capt. F.P. Wye attached RAHQ as Brigade Major. Lt. W. Roberts returned from Signalling Course. Laid out new night lines for all guns on order Group Commander.	
"	25		Three horses returned to M.V.S. in lieu of new Buglers received. Worked night and day on tracks for O.P. now well ahead of 2 R.E. Buglers there. S.O.C.R.A. visited O.P.	
"	26		2nd Lt. W.D. HART 29th Div. temporarily attached to Batty.	
"	27		Registering all day from 3 O.P.s for Raid Barrage	
"	28	11:30pm	Barrage reported very good.	
"	29		Successful and carried out. 2nd Lt Hart N.C.O. Observer shooting under instruction. Very dull & misty all day.	
"	30	6pm	Heavy hostile movements on BOESINGHE. Work on Sun file proceeded, but hung up for labour.	
			Very clear day registered many new targets. Hostile movements very active during evening & Group retaliated. All paths at Belset camouflaged.	

During the week work proceeded on O.P. double wall - now 4'6" high.
Fired 349 rounds during period of 8 days.

2nd Lt Ranaley in charge Wagon line. Work done there include new water troughs with long length of piping pump erected; Lanning of new hut; new hut; road to water trough. During Reading Room for men completed work continued on Billets, standings, roofing.

W Roberts
Lt
OC/D/119/RFA

S E C R E T.   Copy. No. 14

OPERATION ORDER NO. 1 BY LIEUT., COL., P.J.PATERSON D. S. O.,
R. F. A., COMMANDING RIGHT GROUP R.F.A., 38th DIV., ARTILLERY.

Headquarters   Tuesday   9th October 1916.

(1) **INFORMATION.**
A party of the 13th Welsh Regiment is to raid the enemy trenches on the night 12/13th October, entering the hostile trenches at C.22.a.21.71, and bombing for a distance of 40 yards on each side.

(2) **INTENTION.**
Right Group Artillery (Batteries concerned) will assist the operation -
(a) By giving one salvo each at zero time and at zero + 30 secs.
(b) To form a pocket at zero + 8 mins. to prevent interference with the raid.

(3) The following Batteries of the Right Group will fire as under :-
```
"C"-119: 1 How  -  on C.22.a.45.78.
         1  "   -     C.22.a.45.69.
         1  "   -     C.22.a.05.95.
         1  "   -     HAMPSHIRE FARM - C.22.a.86.93.
"C"-122, 2 18 pdrs. on C.22.a.15.85 & C.22.a.15.95.
         2  "      -  Enemy Support-Line immediately
                      in rear of C.22.a.15.85 and
                      C.22.a.15.95.
         2  "      -  Enemy Support-Line from
                      C.22.a.20.95 to C.22.a.43.93.
"C"-121. 6  "      -  From C.22.a.45.78 to
                      C.22.a.58.60.
```

(4) **TIME TABLE.**
All guns fire one round per gun on their objectives at zero time, and at zero + 30 secs., under cover of which the raiding party will advance.
At zero + 8 mins. fire will be opened by "C"-119, "C"-122 and "C"-121 on the above objectives; rate of fire 3 rds. per gun per minute, continuing to zero + 25 minutes when fire will slacken down. At zero + 30 minutes fire will cease.
"A"-122 will fire 3 salvoes at zero-time; 3 salvoes at zero + 30 secs., and 3 salvoes at zero + 8 mins. on Front Line Trench between C.22.b.3.2. and C.22.b.2.3.

(5) 2/Lieut. J.H. Rimmer will act as Liaison Officer. He will be accompanied by two telephonists, and will remain with the Officer i/c of the Raid Party at C.22.a.20.15. He will arrange telephonic and visual communication from this point to "C"-121 O.P.

(6) All Batteries of the Right Group R.F.A. will arrange to have Officers at the O.Ps. on the night 12/13th.

(7) The Liaison Officer will make every effort to send information back to the Right Group.

(8) All watches will be synchronised at RIGHT BRIGADE H-Qrs. at 7 pm. 12th inst, when zero time will be given out.

Copy No. 1 Filed; No 2- R.A.;
3 - Inf. Bde: 4 - O.i/c Raiding   Lieut., Col., R.F.A.
Party; No 5 - 13th Welsh: No.6   Commanding Right Group R.F.A.
to 11 Right Group Batteries;
No. 12 2/Lt. J.H.Rimmer; Nos.13
and 14 War Diary.

S E C R E T.   Copy. No. 7......

OPERATION ORDER NO. 2 BY LIEUT. COL., P.J.PATERSON D.S.O.,
R.F.A., COMMANDING RIGHT GROUP R.F.A. 38th DIV., ARTILLERY.

Headquarters   Tuesday   10th October 1916.

(1) **INFORMATION**.

On the night 12th/13th October 1916 a Raiding Party of the 15th Battalion Welsh Regiment are to investigate enemy sap - Point of entry being C.15.d.25.5. (about)

(2) **INTENTION**.

Right Group Artillery Batteries concerned will be ready to give a Barrage should it be called for.

(3) 2/Lieut. S.R.BONES will act as Liaison Officer and will remain with Col. PARKINSON of the 15th Battalion Welsh Regiment in advanced report centre - ATLAS TRENCH : C.15.c.5½.1. He will be accompanied by two telephonists and will arrange visual and telephonic communication with "C" Battery, 119th Brigade, O.P. Should a Barrage be called for 2/Lieut. S.R. BONES, in consultation with COL. PARKINSON, will pass the code letters A.B. to Officer i/c "C" Battery, 119th Brigade, O.P., who will pass it to "C" Battery, 122nd Brigade, O.P.

The following Batteries will then open fire :-

"C"-122 - 2 18 pdrs. - on Trench: C.15.d.0.8. to
                          C.15.d.3.0.
                        - C.15.d.5.6. towards CANADIAN FARM.
"C"-119 - 2 Hows.   - on C.15.d.6.5.
            1   - C.15.c.9.8.
            1   - C.15.d.5.8.

The Liaison Officer will do his best to send back any information to Group. Watches to be synchronised at LEFT BATTALION HEADQUARTERS at time to be notified later.

Zero time will also be notified later

Rate of fire to commence. 3 rounds per gun per minute, and subsequently, as ordered.

                                        Lieut. Col., R.F.A.
                                Commanding Right Group R.F.A.

Copy. No 1 Filed.
   "   " 2 R.A., 38th Div.
   "   " 3 "C"-119.
   "   " 4 "C"-122.
   "   " 5 2/Lieut. BONES.
   "   " 6 O.C. 15th Battalion Welsh Rgt.
   "   " 7 War Diary.
   "   " 8

Army Form C. 2118

Map. Ref. Sheet 28 BELGIUM 1/40,000
Vol 11

WAR DIARY
or
INTELLIGENCE SUMMARY
(Erase heading not required.) 119th Brigade R.F.A.

Place	Date	Hour	Summary of Events and Information	Remarks and references to Appendices
REGERSBURG	1.10.16		Nothing to report. Enemy very quiet with arty —	W.D.O.
"	2.10.16 to 5.10.16		Nothing to report	W.D.O.
"	6.10.16		A little more hostile activity	W.D.O.
"	7.10.16		Quiet day	W.D.O.
"	8.10.16		Preparations carried out for the raids on Enemy trenches — Enemy more active than usual	W.D.O.
"	9.10.16		Copy of Operation Orders in connection with raid on 12/13 attached	W.D.O.
"	10.10.16		Enemy slightly more active	W.D.O.
"	11.10.16		Nothing to report.	W.D.O.
"	12.10.16 to 13.10.16		Raids carried out as per orders during night of 12th & morning of 13th —	W.D.O.
"	14.10.16 to 15.10.16		Very quiet — on both sides	W.D.O.

WAR DIARY
or
INTELLIGENCE SUMMARY

Army Form C. 2118

War Ref. Sheet 27 BELGIUM 1/40,000
" " " 28 " "

(Erase heading not required.)

Place	Date	Hour	Summary of Events and Information	Remarks and references to Appendices
Regersburg	16.10.16 to 21.10.16		Quiet period.	WDE WDE
"	22.10.16		A little more activity on both sides	WDE
"	23.10.16		Other schemes of raids were drawn up but are held in abeyance	WDE
"	24.10.16		The retaliated with Howitzers for shelling of front line	WDE
"	25.10.16 to 27.10.16		Nothing to report	WDE
"	28.10.16		Nothing to report	
"	29.10.16		Received orders that Brigade Hqrs will be relieved in action by 122 Brigade R.F.A. on 30.10.16.	WDE
HAMMOEK	30.10.16		Bde. Hqrs moved back to Wagon Lines located at F.18.c.4.4 (Sheet 27) on afternoon and night of 30th.	WDE
"	31.10.16		Nothing to report	WDE

Major H.9? R.F.A.
Comdg 119/R.F.A.

WAR DIARY or INTELLIGENCE SUMMARY.

Army Form C. 2118

A/119th Brigade. R.F.A.

Place	Date	Hour	Summary of Events and Information	Remarks and references to Appendices
DAWSON'S CORNER. B.22.d.1.8. Sheet 28.	1st Oct 1916		Battery still in action under 2nd Lieut Pringle RFA. Comdg. Left Group R.F.A.	
	10/4/16		Lieut P. Carrier. R.F.A. (T.F.) posted to Battery	
	11/4/16		Right Section Guns moved to forward position during night.	
	12/4/16		Battery in action at night covering raiding party of 13th R.W.F. Raid successful. Machine gun & prisoner captured	
	13/4/16		do do 15th R.W.F. Raid successful. 4 prisoners captured	
	14/4/16		2nd Lieut Donovan proceeded on 10 days leave to England	
	15/4/16		Right Section Guns brought back from forward position at night	
	16/4/16		Fired 150 rds & breached German parapet, in conjunction with B & D Batteries 119th Bde. R.F.A.	
	18/4/16		Lieut P. Carrier RFA (T.F) posted to 13/119	
	19/4/16		Lieut J.C. Griffiths posted to Battery from B/119. Lieut. Carrier. R.F.A (T.F.) posted to 13/119	
			Capt. C. a Rhyn went on leave to England — for 10 days. Lieut J.C. Griffiths assumes temporary command of Battery	
	21/4/16		2nd Lieut Donovan returns from leave	
	28/4/16		Fired 12 S rds & breached forward parapet. Centre Section Guns taken to forward position.	
	29/4/16		Capt C. a Rhyn returns from leave. Battery in action at night covering raiding party of 15th R.W.F. Raid successful. 3 prisoners captured.	
	30/4/16		Centre Section Guns brought back from forward position	

C. Rhyn
CAPT. R.F.A.
COMDG. "A" BATTERY, R.F.A.
119th BRIGADE, R.F.A.

WAR DIARY of B/119 BDE RFA
INTELLIGENCE SUMMARY

Army Form C. 2118

(Erase heading not required.)

Place	Date	Hour	Summary of Events and Information	Remarks and references to Appendices
BRIELEN B.29.B.6.6	1st 1/10/16	3:30pm	Fired 6 rounds at M.G. firing at aeroplane C14 a 2½.8.	Ref Sheet 28 N.W.2. Bel. 3.E. Eaw.
	2nd		Nil	Eaw.
	3rd	3pm	Fired 1/2 " " "	"
	4th		Nil	
	5th	2:30pm	Fired 2 rounds at 2 observers looking over parapet at C14 a 3.5 — Disappeared	Eaw
	6th	7am	Dispersed working parties C14 B 25.45 and C14 b 1.3 (4+10 rounds)	
		8:45am	" "	2do
			Hostile artillery day inactive than usual, firing scattered & no apparent definite object.	Eaw
	7th		Nil	Eaw. Eaw.
	8th		Nil	Eaw. Eaw.
	9th	4am	Fired 17 rounds at two observers at C14 a 2.8½ disappeared	Eaw.
		9.10	" 8 rounds at working party C14 a 5.9	Eaw.
	10th		Dispersed working party at C14 a 3.3 with 4 rounds	Eaw
	11th		Nil	

WAR DIARY of B/119 BDE RFA

or

INTELLIGENCE SUMMARY

(Erase heading not required.)

Army Form C. 2118

Instructions regarding War Diaries and Intelligence Summaries are contained in F.S. Regs., Part II. and the Staff Manual respectively. Title Pages will be prepared in manuscript.

Place	Date	Hour	Summary of Events and Information	Remarks and references to Appendices
BRIELEN B28B8.6	12/10/16	9am	Operations in connection with raid by 13th R.I.F. on trench at C14 a 4½.2	Ref Sheet 28 N.W. 2. Ed 3.E
		9.13pm	Bombardment 4 guns C14 a 5.2 – C14 a 3¾.4 Enfilade Xn at C28.C3½ on support trench C14 a 6½ – C14 a 5.3¾ at Xn fire 5 sec.	
		9.3pm	Raiders entered enemy trench.	
		9.3pm	Barrage 2 guns C14 a 3.4 to C14 a 4.5½ at X fire 15 rounds 2 guns (enfilade) C14 a 6.2½ – C14 a 5.3¾ at Xn fire 10 rounds	
		9.27pm	Raiders captured 1 prisoner and 1 M.G. – Total expenditure on raid – 233 rounds	Ammo.
	13/10/16	10am	Cut wire at C13B95.7.8 fired 113 rounds grps of 15 yds cuts in which wire –	
		8.14 – 6.14pm	Bombardment for raid by 15th R.I.V.F on C13.B95.77 enfilade Xn on C14 a 1½.5 3/8 – C14 a ½.7¼ at Xn fire 5 sec.	
		6.14pm – about 9pm	2 guns C14 a 17 – C14 a 2½.8. 2 guns C14 a 8½.8 to C7.C.93.1 2 guns enfilade C14 a 25.8 – C14 a 11.9½ – at Xn fire 10 rounds Total expenditure 456 rounds. – Raid successful 8 prisoners captured	Ammo.

WAR DIARY of B/119 BDE RFA

INTELLIGENCE SUMMARY
(Erase heading not required.)

Army Form C. 2118

Instructions regarding War Diaries and Intelligence Summaries are contained in F.S. Regs., Part II. and the Staff Manual respectively. Title Pages will be prepared in manuscript.

Place	Date	Hour	Summary of Events and Information	Remarks and references to Appendices
BRIELEN. B28 B6.6	14th 10/16	1 am	Fired 20 rounds at C14a 2.5 retaliation for enemy T.M.S.	Ref. Sheet 28 N.W. 2. Ed 3.E.
	15th	6 am	" 15 " " "	
		11.0 am –12.15 p	Shelled C14a 30.35 USA destroy parapet and damage wire in conjunction with 4.5 Howtzr. Fired 150 rounds NS Successful-parapet flattened for about 20 yds	
			4 rounds C14a.17	
		3 pm 4.30 p	Fired 40 rounds retaliation for enemy T.M's Hostile artillery active —	Enw –
	16th		hit	Enw
	17th	11.30 am	Fired 7 rounds C14 a 2.5 suspected position of M.G firing on aeroplane.	
		12 noon	4 rounds C14 a 17 to find error of day	
		12.45 p –3 pm	200 rounds C14a 1.3 6½ in conjunction with 4 Show to destroy parapet and damage wire. Parapet seriously damaged for about 40 yds – wire U/D implacement damaged knocked about and small gun ent	
		5.30 p –6 p	Fired 20 rds with enfilade Xm at C13 9.3 under order from left group	Enw.

1875 Wt. W593/826 1,000,000 4/15 J.B.C. & A. A.D.S.S./Forms/C. 2118.

Army Form C. 2118

WAR DIARY of 13/149 BDE RFA
or
INTELLIGENCE SUMMARY
(Erase heading not required.)

Instructions regarding War Diaries and Intelligence Summaries are contained in F.S. Regs., Part II. and the Staff Manual respectively. Title Pages will be prepared in manuscript.

Place	Date	Hour	Summary of Events and Information	Remarks and references to Appendices
BRIELEN B26c36.6	18th	3.30	Fired 20 rounds C14 a 2.5 in retaliation for minenwerfer	Ref Sheet 28 NW 2 Ed 3 E
	19th	—	" 10 rounds C7 a 5.2 by order of 2 gp group	
		9.20p	Dispersed working party at C14 a 16.95 with 9 rounds	(A)
	19th	6am	" " " C14 a 5.5 " "	
	20th	10.20a 4.2 pm	" " " C14 a 15.95	(B)
		11.30am	Calibrated on KOLN FM 13.tds	
	21st		Nil	(C)
	22nd	6.30pm 6.30pm 6.45pm	Fired 56 rounds on C14 n 8.6, C14 a 2.5, C8 c 10 in retaliation for minenwerfer	(D)
	23rd	9am 5pm	Dispersed working party at C14 a 3½, 3½ " 20 rounds at C14 a 2.5 & C9 c 10 retaliation for minenwerfer	(E)
	24th 25th		Nil Nil	
	26th	5.30p 5.30p	5.50pm—55b fired Hoverned enfilading trench C7 a 5.2 — C7 a 2.3 covering TM fire	(F)
	27th	11.45	Dispersed working party C14 a 1½, 9 a 12 rds	(G)

1875 Wt. W593/826 1,000,000 4/15 J.B.C. & A. A.D.S.S./Forms/C. 2118.

WAR DIARY of B/119 A.D.E. R.F.A.
INTELLIGENCE SUMMARY

Army Form C. 2118

Instructions regarding War Diaries and Intelligence Summaries are contained in F.S. Regs., Part II. and the Staff Manual respectively. Title Pages will be prepared in manuscript.

(Erase heading not required.)

Place	Date	Hour	Summary of Events and Information	Remarks and references to Appendices
BRIELEN B28 B8 6	28/10/16	11.30am -3pm	Fired in conjunction with A/119 (18pdr) & D/119 (how) 125 rounds on enemy trench at C14a 3½.3½ — Trench badly damaged.	Ref Sheet 28NW.2 Ed 3 E
		3pm -3.35pm	Fired 51 rounds covering T.M.S	Enemy
	29/10/16	3pm -3.20pm	Fired 100 rounds in conjunction with 6 hows as demonstration at C14a @ 6½ Parapet much damaged	
		11.24pm -11.29pm	2 guns (enfilade) bombarded front line C7c69 — C7c68 in conjunction with raid by 16th RWF on C7c67. Rate of fire 1m fire 5 secs.	
		11.24pm -11.29pm	Barrage C7d 1.7 — C7c 9.7½ at 3 rounds per gun per minute — Raid successful 3 prisoners and 3 slight casualties —	Enemy
	30/10/16		Nil.	
	31/10/16	30 12 noon	Nil	Enemy

Wood
Capt
Cmdg B/119 A.D.E. R.F.A.

Army Form C. 2118

D. Batenfield
119 Bde RFA

WAR DIARY
or
INTELLIGENCE SUMMARY
(Erase heading not required.)

Instructions regarding War Diaries and Intelligence Summaries are contained in F.S. Regs., Part II. and the Staff Manual respectively. Title Pages will be prepared in manuscript.

Place	Date	Hour	Summary of Events and Information	Remarks and references to Appendices
"GHENT COTTAGES" BRIELEN	October 1st to 5th		The enemy artillery were only moderately active, but their trench Mortars were in continual use against the Belgians and our Left Battalion. No 3 Gun was moved into the New Emplacement which had been constructed for it in the new rear section position by the BRIELEN – ELVERDINGHE	Minut.
	6th to 10th		Slightly more hostile artillery activity, but nothing of heavier calibre than 10.5 cm howitzer: hostile Trench Mortars maintained their activity and calls for retaliation fairly frequent. 1emp 2nd Lt Hart RFA reported 29th Divl Artillery on 9th inst	Minut.
	11th	2pm	2nd Lt M.T. Webster R.F.A. (TF) joined posted from 55th Divl Artillery	Minut.
	12th	9pm	Supported raid by 13th RWF on German Line trenches just NW of KRUPP SALIENT. One machine gun and one prisoner captured.	Minut.
	13	8pm	Supported successful raid by 15th RWF on German front line trenches near CEASARS NOSE SALIENT on PILCKEM RIDGE. 4 prisoners captured.	Minut.
	14		Retaliated for hostile T.M. activity	Minut.
	15		Fired 100 rounds at German Front Line near KRUPP SALIENT. Hostile retaliation feeble. Much damage done to enemy trench.	Minut.
	11th to 15th		Hostile artillery less active generally, but trench mortars occasions frequent retaliation	Minut.
	16th to 20th		Occasional 77mm and 10.5 cm batteries active. Hostile T.M's active daily especially against CANAL BANK on the 16th inst	Minut.

WAR DIARY or INTELLIGENCE SUMMARY

Army Form C. 2118

(Erase heading not required.)

Place	Date	Hour	Summary of Events and Information	Remarks and references to Appendices
	19th	2.00am	100 rounds fired into hostile front line at (?) a 1½ b 6½ (Sheet 36) Parapet (reached trench) heavily damaged. Enemy retaliated with about 30 10.5 cm (How) rounds close to forward Echelon. 1 N.C.O. slightly wounded, otherwise no damage done. Hostile fire was probably directed on old & Howitzer position close to forward echelon and shot from register.	Apdx
	21st & 25th		Hostile MINNENWERFER were especially active on 23rd inst between 6 and 7 p.m. Battery fired group retaliation programme & known and combined programme RIGHT and LEFT Groups once. 3 targets were registered with aeroplane during the day, but wind was too strong for steady shooting. Low light owing to mist and rain made observation poor during the remaining three days. Two howitzers borrowed from D/121 Bde. R.F.A. brought into action on evening 25th inst. Two howitzers withdrawn and sent for repair on 26th inst.	Apdx
	26th		Light for observation fair only.	Apdx
	"	5.30pm	Battery fired 40 rounds at (?) y0 b.7 and B12½ 9.8 to cover our own trench mortar fire. Hostile retaliation feeble.	Apdx
	27th		Hostile light field howitzer active on Left Battalion trenches. Battery retaliated for this and for bombing by Heavy T.M. on enemy front line trenches and works about FARM.nt.	Apdx
	28th	11.30am 12 noon	100 rounds fired at C½ a 3½ & previously fired on 15th inst. Parapet again trenched and trenches again damaged, much material thrown up. High wind interfered with accuracy of shooting.	Apdx

Army Form C. 2118

WAR DIARY
or
INTELLIGENCE SUMMARY
(Erase heading not required.)

Instructions regarding War Diaries and Intelligence Summaries are contained in F. S. Regs., Part II. and the Staff Manual respectively. Title Pages will be prepared in manuscript.

Place	Date	Hour	Summary of Events and Information	Remarks and references to Appendices
	28th	3 to 3.35 pm	Fired on B12,6,9,8 Trenches to cover our trench mortar fire: trenches damaged.	Appx
	29th	12.30 to 1pm	Considerable trench mortar activity against our Left Batt: and Right Batt: trenches. Retaliated 3 times according to Group programme.	Appx
		3 pm	Fired 50 rounds into hostile front line at C.14.a.1½.6½ breaching parapet and destroying repair work done by enemy after shoot on 17th inst. at this point.	
	29th 30th	11.20 pm 12.25 am	Fired on C.9c.9¾.7¾ and C.9.3.3½.9½ according to Left Group Operation Order to cover raid by 16th Battn R.W.F. on enemy front line salient at C.9.6.7 which was succeeded. 3 prisoners being brought in.	Appx
	30		Light frost all day owing to rain	Appx
	31		Hostile artillery slightly active.	Appx
			Two guns (howrs) brought into action again on completion of repairs. Two howitzers belonging to D/121 Bge R.F.A. returned to their wagon line.	Appx

[signature] Capt.
Commanding D. Ba[...]
119th Brigade R.F.A.

WAR DIARY
INTELLIGENCE SUMMARY.

Army Form C. 2118.

Place	Date	Hour	Summary of Events and Information	Remarks and references to Appendices
HAMHOEK	1.11.16 to 28.11.16		Bde. Hqrs. remained at rest in Wagon Lines. Work was carried on there improving accommodation for Officers & Men and building models, shams &c. Btys. remained in Action (see Bty. Diaries attached)	WDR
TROISTOURS	29.11.16		Lt-Col. Paterson relieved of Lt. Col. Pringle in Command of the Left Group - consisting of A/119, B/119, D/119, A/121, B/121, D/121. C/119 in Action in Right Group	WDR
"	30.11.16		Bde. Hqrs. moved up and completed relief of Bde. Hqrs. of 121/R.F.A.	WDR

Watson
Lt-Col. R.F.A.
Comdg 119th Brigade R.F.A.

WAR DIARY
INTELLIGENCE SUMMARY
(Erase heading not required.)

Army Form C. 2118

Place	Date	Hour	Summary of Events and Information	Remarks and references to Appendices
Dawson's Corner. B.22.d. Sheet 28 NW	November 1st		Battery still in action at Dawson's Corner. Lt. Col. Prinsep D.S.O. commanding. Left Group R.H.A.	
	7th		C.R.A. 38th Div. inspected Battery position	
	9th		Enemy more active to-day. Besides usual targets, Battery fired a good deal in retaliation.	
	13th		G.O.C. 38th Div. & C.R.A. 38th Div. inspected the Battery position.	
	14th		2/Lieut. S.S. Clarke proceeded on 10 days' leave to England. Lieut. J.C. Griffiths came up from wagon lines to Gun Position. Battery registered on Caledonia Trench (High Command) in conjunction with Right Group R.F.A. in preparation for coming raid.	
	15th		Registration on High Command carried on.	
	16th		Battery took part in a 1 hour bombardment of High Command.	
	17th		Battery took part in bombardment & fire covering raiding party of 14 & Welch on High Command Redoubt. Raid completely successful. Lieut. J.C. Griffiths left for course in England.	
	18th		Battery commenced registering on its shooting in connection with Raid.	
	19th		Representation of Battery attended parade before Corps Commander of Raiding Party & R.A. taking part, to receive his congratulations on success of raid. 2/Lieut. Turner (A/121) loaned to the Battery for a few days.	
	23rd		2/Lieut. Turner returned to his Battery to-day.	
	27th		2/Lieut. S.S. Clarke returned from leave to-day. 2/Lieut. R. Sealey arrived from England posted to the Battery.	

[signature] Capt., R.F.A.
Comdg. "A" Battery, R.F.A.
119th Brigade, R.F.A.

Army Form C. 2118

WAR DIARY of B/49 BDE RFA
or
INTELLIGENCE SUMMARY
(Erase heading not required.)

Instructions regarding War Diaries and Intelligence Summaries are contained in F.S. Regs., Part II. and the Staff Manual respectively. Title Pages will be prepared in manuscript.

Place	Date	Hour	Summary of Events and Information	Remarks and references to Appendices
BRIELEN B25 B8.6	1/11/16	11.14 am	Fired 20 rounds C14 B 51.6 in retaliation for minenwerfer	Ref 28.IW.2. 5th JULGN 9/40000 Ed SE.
		12 noon	" " "	
		2.20 pm & 3.58 pm	Dispersed working parties at C14 a 2.8 — with 11 rounds	
	2/11/16	2.5 pm & 3.40 pm	Dispersed working parties at C14 a 2.8 with 10 rounds	
			— firing at C14 a 5.9	
	3/11/16	10.30 am	10 rounds at C14 a 2.7½ in retaliation for minenwerfer	
		11 am	Fired 10 rounds registration for special shoot on C14 a 3.4.	
		1.15 pm	Shi[?] W.P. at C14 a 5.9 with 12 rounds	
	4/11/16	Afternoon	Fired 12 rounds to disperse working party at C14 a 3.5	
	5/11/16	11 am 6.30 am	Fired 120 rounds on C14 a 2.4 in retaliation for enemy shelling	
			Burnage [?] parapet & wire erected	
	6/11/16	10.55 am 4.45 am	Fired 6 rounds on C7 a 2.6 in destruction shoot for T.M.'s	
			— rounds C14 B 5½.6 retaliation for T.M.'s	
		4 pm & 5.20 pm	Dispersed working parties at C14 a 2.8 & 3¼ & C14 a 5 & Z.1.9.7	

1875 Wt. W593/826 1,000,000 4/15 J.B.C. & A. A.D.S.S./Forms/C. 2118.

Army Form C. 2118

WAR DIARY of B/ing Bde RFA
or
INTELLIGENCE SUMMARY

(Erase heading not required.)

Place	Date	Hour	Summary of Events and Information	Remarks and references to Appendices
BRIELEN N.17346	7/4/16	5pm	20 rounds retaliation on C14 b 5½.6 retaliation for TM's	Ref 20 MW 2. ST JULIEN t/1000 Ed 3E Zero
	8/4/16	9.15am	dispersed W.P. at C14 a 4½.4½ with 10 rounds.	
	9/4/16	12.20pm	10 hits on C14 a 8.7½ in retaliation for RM's —	
		2.15pm	dispersed WP. C.14 a 6.9 with 12 rds.	
		2.55pm	20 rounds at C14 a 3½.4 in retaliation for shelling	
		5pm	16 rounds searching for TM smoke of discharge enable position estimated probably at C15c 4½.0.	Zero
	10/4/16	9.60am	11 rds to disperse W.P. at C14 a 3½.4	
		11am	27 rds at loophole plate C13 90.75 head hit but loophole not destroyed —	
		12.45pm	first rounds retaliation to C14 a 3½.4	Zero
	11/4/16	3pm	fired rounds. at C14 a 9.2½ in retaliation for TM. fire	
		3am	fired 96 rounds German front line from C157 y.8 — C14 a 3½.4 E.C. right lines under our LEFT GROUP. as reply to Enemy shelling shellies on front line opposite —	
		12 noon	10 rounds C14 a 8.2½ retaliation for TM fire	
		1pm		
		3.40pm	22 rounds dispersing German working parties C16c 3.9, C14 a 25.6 & C14 a 4.5½	Zero
		7.20pm		

Army Form C. 2118

D. Bolton
1/12/56 R.F.H.

WAR DIARY
on
INTELLIGENCE SUMMARY
(Erase heading not required.)

Instructions regarding War Diaries and Intelligence Summaries are contained in F.S. Regs., Part II. and the Staff Manual respectively. Title Pages will be prepared in manuscript.

Place	Date	Hour	Summary of Events and Information	Remarks and references to Appendices
"GHENT COTTAGES" BRIELEN.	October 1st/10	5ᵖ	The enemy artillery were only moderately active, but their Trench Mortars were in continual use against the Belgians and our Left Battalion. No.3 gun was moved into the new emplacement which had been constructed for it in the new rear section position by the BRIELEN-ELVERDINGHE road.	1/k
"	6th/10	10ᵃ	Slightly more hostile artillery, but nothing of heavier calibre than 10.5 cm howitzer. Hostile trench mortars maintained their activity, calls for retaliation fairly frequent. Temp L. Hoult R.F.A. rejoined 29th Divl Artillery on 9th inst.	2/k
"	11th	"	2 A.M. Webster R.F.A. (T.F.) joined, posted from 55th Divl Artillery.	3/k
"	12th	9pm	Supported raid by 13th R.W.F. on German trench line trenches just N.W. of KRUPP SALIENT. One Machine gun and one Prisoner captured.	4/k
"	13th		Congratulatory message on above forwarded to Lt. Col. Garnett Commanding 13th Bn.	5/k
"	13th	8pm	Supported successful raid by 15th R.W.F. on German front line trenches near CEASARS NOSE salient on PIXEN ridge. 4 Prisoners captured.	6/k
"	14th		Approx. 100 rounds L.V. assistance to raid given by left group. Germans retired from L.G. to R.W.F. retaliated for hostile T.M. activity.	7/k
"	15th		Fired 100 rounds at German front line near KRUPP SALIENT. Hostile retaliation weak though damage close to enemy trench.	8/k
"	17th/10	15ᵃ	Hostile artillery slow active generally, but Trench Mortars maintained frequent retaliation.	9/k

WAR DIARY or INTELLIGENCE SUMMARY

Army Form C. 2118

(Erase heading not required.)

Instructions regarding War Diaries and Intelligence Summaries are contained in F.S. Regs., Part II. and the Staff Manual respectively. Title Pages will be prepared in manuscript.

Place	Date	Hour	Summary of Events and Information	Remarks and references to Appendices
	15th	20th	Occasional T.M. and 10·5 c.m. Batteries active. Hostile T.M.'s active daily, especially against K. CAPHR BRNK and 187 inst.	J.R.
	17th	noon	100 rounds fired in 6 hostile front line at C.M. a.v. 6/4 Sheet 28. Parapet breached. Hostile sentry damaged. Enemy retaliated with about 20 10·5 c.m. Howr rounds close to forward seen one N.C.O. slightly wounded & traverse no damage done. Hostile fire was probably directed on old & Hawtige position close to forward see min. and shot from register.	J.R.
	21st to 25th		Two Lt. MINNENWERFER were especially active on 22nd inst. Usual [?] and T.M. Battery fired groups retaliation and countered programme. Right and Left groups met. 3 Targets were registered with assistance during the day. Hot wind was too strong for steady shooting. Poor light owing to mist and rain made observation poor during the remaining of the days. Our hostige barraged from star Bett. R.F.A. hung to action in evening of 25th inst. No howitzers withdrawn sent to T.C.W. for repair on 26th.	J.R.
	26th		Light job observation fair only.	
		5·30 pm	Battery fired 40 rounds at C.7.C.6.7 and 13.12.6.9.8 to cover our own [?] mortar fire. Hostile retaliation [?].	J.R.
	27th		Hostile Light Field Howitzers active on Left battalion trenches. Battery retaliated for this and fire from [?] by Heavy T.M. on enemy front line trenches and works about farm 14.	J.R.
	28th	11·30 am / 12 noon	100 rounds fired at C.M. a. 3/2.4. previously fired at on 15th inst. Parapet again breached and trenches again damaged much material thrown up. High wind interfered with accuracy of shooting.	J.R.
		3/6 3·25 pm	Fired on R.12.b. g.8. trenches. Own [?] mortar fire, trenches damaged.	J.R.
	29th	12·30 am / 1 am	Considerable trench mortar activity against our Left Battn. & Right Battn. trenches. Retaliated 3 times according to Group Programme.	J.R.
		3 pm	Fired 30 rounds in 6 hostile front line at C.M. a. 1/2. 6/2. breaching parapet and disturbing repair work done by enemy at 16 [?] on 17th inst at this point.	J.R.

1875 Wt. W593/826 1,000,000 4/15 J.B.C. & A. A.D.S.S./Forms/C. 2118.

Instructions regarding War Diaries and Intelligence Summaries are contained in F. S. Regs., Part II. and the Staff Manual respectively. Title Pages will be prepared in manuscript.

WAR DIARY
or
INTELLIGENCE SUMMARY
(Erase heading not required.)

Army Form C. 2118

Place	Date	Hour	Summary of Events and Information	Remarks and references to Appendices
	29th	11.20pm	Fired on C.7.C.9¾.7¾ and C.7.C.1½.9½ according to Left Group Operation Order to cover raid by 16th Battn R.W.F on enemy front line salient at C.7.C.6.7, which was successful 3 prisoners being brought in.	F.
	30th	12.25am		
	"		Light (Vis). poor all day owing to rain.	F.
	31st		Hostile Artillery slightly active	
	"	"	Two guns (Hows) brought into action again on completion of repairs. Two Howitzers belonging to D/121 Bde R.F.A. returned to their wagon line	F.

F. P. Wye
Capt
Comdg D/119 Bde R.F.A.

1875 Wt. W593/826 1,000,000 4/15 J.B.C. & A. A.D.S.S./Forms/C. 2118.

Army Form C. 2118.

WAR DIARY
or
INTELLIGENCE SUMMARY.
(Erase heading not required.)

D/119 Brigade R.F.A.

Hour, Date, Place	Summary of Events and Information	Remarks and references to Appendices
Battery H.Q. at GHENT COTTAGES BRIELEN. Right Section in action at B.22.d.90.65. Left Section in action at B.22.d.4.3. O.P. at TWIN COTS (south) B.19.b.1.3	**1916**	
Nov 1.	Good light for observation throughout day. Gas shells fired about 30 yards behind 10 and 11 am Batteries on BRIELEN with light and 2 medium T.M. for which the Batteries were freed. MINNIE retaliation under orders from J.F. Group. 12 Spot one 17 and 10 inch Howitzers opened fire on VON MOLTKE redoubt also PICKEM fired 25 rounds firing about 4.30 pm. About 5 pm enemy retaliated on CAPPER FARM and trenches in C9a with 7.5 cm howitzers and some 10.5 field Batteries (77 mm) at 5.15 pm and 5.35 pm the Railway fired rounds from salvos in retaliation. A quiet night.	
Nov 2.	O.P. on Rear Section position entered, spaces between elements not touched in and cemented in front of pits to stop bombardment of steel penetrating between roofs.	
Nov 3.	Rendered worth aeroplane flight T.M. fire to Germans from howitzer on VON MOLTKE redoubt in afternoon drawing heavy retaliation for which we retaliated.	
" 4.	Slight activity by T.M's the retaliated.	
" 5.	Quiet day. Hostile working party dispersed.	
" 6.	6.42 horses posted to the Battery which us now up to strength. Considerable service fire on our front line about 8 am. Counter barrage. We retaliated and about 10.45 am bombarded VON MOLTKE redoubt by DICTAT in retaliation of shoot by our 6 in Howitzers. Rather hostile fire.	
" 7.	Heavy rain.	
" 8.	Quiet day. Capt. J. feslie R.F.A. to England on leave. I reported to advance command.	

(73989) W.4141—463. 400,000. 9/14. H.&J.Ltd. Forms/C. 2118/10.

WAR DIARY
INTELLIGENCE SUMMARY.
(Erase heading not required.)

Army Form C. 2118.

Instructions regarding War Diaries and Intelligence Summaries are contained in F.S. Regs., Part II. and the Staff Manual respectively. Title pages will be prepared in manuscript.

Hour, Date, Place	Summary of Events and Information	Remarks and references to Appendices
Nov 9	Engaged other battery 9.30am. Heavy Retaliation from Group Zm during day. BOMBARD also present.	
10	About 1.30pm about 10-11cm fell in neighbourhood of bheer. About 6 rounds and some very near.	
11	11pm. Fired about 60 rounds with TMs. Kreo and 18 below at Front Line Gyst 70 FORMN.1. Bombardment reported effective by Infantry. Infantry at PICKEM Ordered today to attack on orders from Group.	
12	Misty day. Recce Col Haigle inspected the position.	
13	1am. Retaliated twice for Mortars. Very boggy morning 11am. GOC Sherman and GOC RA. Col Haigle inspected position pm & Relief. Sat working to complain of Right good in afternoon	
14	Hudson shot at MAUSER COT. Bombarded twice 6am in afternoon. Two new howitzers arrived in evening.	
15	Put two new howitzers in to advance Position to replace two (380 = 299) which had cracked (Callery now constitutes A 1035 RGF 1915 B 1251 1914 C 30 1911 D 305 1916) and	
16	2pm 6.2pm fired 200 rounds front line (as Cu at 317 to Cu at 1) and registered for shoot.	
17	Weather very cold. Engaged two boche batteries during morning. 11.30am 400 rounds on front line as day before in preparation for shoot	

WAR DIARY or INTELLIGENCE SUMMARY

Army Form C. 2118.

(3)

Hour, Date, Place	Summary of Events and Information	Remarks and references to Appendices
Nov 17	5-6.30 pm 200 rounds in preparation for raid.	
	10.59 pm 300 rounds on road on HIGH COMMAND REDOUBT. Ray successful took 20 prisoners.	
18	Very wet and cold. Fired 18 rounds at HOOKER BATTERY. Quiet.	
19	Softener Crops Commence. Congratulations successful raid.	
20	Quiet day. Shot new cannon at Trench Jon.	
21	" " Not engaged	
22	Foggy. Not engaged	
23	Foggy. Not engaged	
	Kent 107 & Cento RFA to England on leave. Lieut NM W-Jones assumes Command. Registered new MINNIE emus (CAREOUS SUPPORT) Registration of new pieces on CANON FARM. Enlarged gap in Enemy Front line at CH4.314	
24	Misty. No hostile fire of any kind.	
25	Heavy mist. Not engaged.	
26	Good shooting day. Destroyed saw roof on FARMS BARRICADE. Trench ten rounds at Front Line Cd 9.1.5 registering for Group shoot on Trench Ten C8 c 2.2.9. Minnenby. from "OP o + 100" to Front line. Breaches parapet at Ch 4 9t.16. MINNIE EQUIP C(2) and ROMBARA by Group order: Also shots on Railways No 3 v1. Decking evening fired a Salvo by Group order at C8c 2.2.4 (last one at 9.20 pm. Knocked retaliation which led to MINNIE-EALING 9 mins.	
27	Aeroplane registration of LOOPER BATTERY No 1 (2nd) between 3 pm + 4.30 pm. BROKEN (?) and MOLTKE: at 1.30 pm Group ordered Salvo on front line Ch a.3 36. Enemy shelled HEAWLEY north TR.5 and 10.5 cm (and) MINNIE-EALING (3) and MINNIE 8 to 8.35 pm Section Line 20 recs on NIGHT LINES	

Army Form C. 2118.

WAR DIARY
or
INTELLIGENCE SUMMARY.
(Erase heading not required.)

Instructions regarding War Diaries and Intelligence Summaries are contained in F.S. Regs., Part II and the Staff Manual respectively. Title pages will be prepared in manuscript.

Hour, Date, Place	Summary of Events and Information	Remarks and references to Appendices
Nov 27	Quiet until 9.20 when we fired by Group Order at "TRENCH" TRAMWAY Cross Sigt. One Casualty. 6 ID.M. Gas overhead.	
28	Foggy	
29	Foggy	
30	Foggy and very cold. IMs apparently from neighbourhood of FARM14. Shelling took place from MRs.	

W.P. Nash

Army Form C. 2118

WAR DIARY
or
INTELLIGENCE SUMMARY

(Erase heading not required.)

of B he Bde RFA (3)

Instructions regarding War Diaries and Intelligence Summaries are contained in F.S. Regs., Part II. and the Staff Manual respectively. Title Pages will be prepared in manuscript.

Place	Date	Hour	Summary of Events and Information	Remarks and references to Appendices
ARIELEN B24/B36 b	12/4/16	10.30 am	Shrapnel working party C14 a 1.9 with 4 rds.	Ref 1/5 NW 2. 1/10000 Col 3E.
		3 pm	Fired 50 rounds at new work C14 a 25·50 – C14 a 10·95 at orders from LEFT GROUP. – much Fuller thrown up.	eau
		4.10 pm	60 rounds at C14 a 36·24 by way of in retaliation for enemy shelling	
	13/4/16	1.15 pm	Fired 30 rounds on C14 a 1.7 retaliation by order	
		2 – 2.30 pm	Fired 16 rounds the supplement fire of 12" How on MOLTKE REDOUBT KOLN FM to catch hostile Garrisons hit	eau
	14/4/16		nil	eau
	15/4/16		nil	eau
	16/4/16	2.3 pm	Let mine at C14 a 35·4. Shooting in enfilade almost direct there – 150 rounds – fairly successful. 6 part of so got out.	
		3.4 pm	Fired 3 00 rounds on C14 on 3.04 – C14 a 1.7 breaking his front line much damage done a several weak places in wire offered into gaps.	
	17/4/16	12 pm	150 rounds were sent thing C14 a 1.7 was very fairly good working throwing have in enfilade – much got out between C14 a 3½ 4 – C14 a 1.7 with bombs from lines C14 a 3.4 and hay retaliation	

1875 Wt. W593/826 1,000,000 4/15 J.B.C. & A. A.D.S.S./Forms/C.2118

Army Form C. 2118

WAR DIARY of B/by Bde R.F.A.
or
INTELLIGENCE SUMMARY

(Erase heading not required.)

Instructions regarding War Diaries and Intelligence Summaries are contained in F.S. Regs., Part II. and the Staff Manual respectively. Title Pages will be prepared in manuscript.

(4)

Place	Date	Hour	Summary of Events and Information	Remarks and references to Appendices
ORIFLEN B26&36	18/4/16	6-6.30 pm	1 section of C14 a 4.6 – C14 a 26.8, one section on C14 a 1.7 – C14 a 27.8 duplicate to C14 a 32.3 – C14 a 4.6 – at 3 rounds per gun per minute Demonstration in connection with Highs command Request by 14th Welsh Regt.	Auth PG840/2 1/10000 3E
		16.54 –11.12pm	Bombardment, 4 guns on C14 a 32.4 – C14 a 1.6 at 6 rounds per gun four minutes.	
		11.12pm –11.5pm	Left – 4 guns C14 a 4.6 – C14 a 1.92 at 4 rounds per gun two min	
		11.5pm –11.40pm	Runny 1 section C14 a 9.0 – C14 D 12.1 one section C14 a 1.7 – C14 a 13.8 Enfilade action C14 a 32.14 – C14 a 4.6 – at 2 hds per gun per min	
		11.40 –11.40pm	1 section C14 a 8.0 – C14 a 93.0, 1 section C14 a 9.0 – C14 b 12.1 at 3 nds per gun per minute	8hrs 2260
	19/4/16		nil	
	19/4/16	10-10.30am	Working parties dispersed at C14 a 32.7 + C14 a 32.4.24 rounds	8hrs
	20/4/16		nil	8hrs

Army Form C. 2118

WAR DIARY
or
INTELLIGENCE SUMMARY

of Bty RFA

(Erase heading not required.)

Instructions regarding War Diaries and Intelligence Summaries are contained in F.S. Regs., Part II. and the Staff Manual respectively. Title Pages will be prepared in manuscript.

Place	Date	Hour	Summary of Events and Information	Remarks and references to Appendices
BRIEFEN. B28 b86	21/11/16		Working parties dispersed at C14a 2.9 - C14a 25.75 with 12 rounds	Elen O
	22/4/16		nil	Elen O
	23/4/16	1.30pm	Fired 12 rounds on front line C3b 9.8 - C14a 3½.4 to cover aeroplane taking photographs	Elen O
	24/4/16	6.30am 4.30pm	Dispersed working parties at C14a 6.0 and C14a 4.5 with 24 rounds	Elen O
	25/4/16		nil	
	26/4/16	11.30am	36 rounds at C14a 9.6. Calibration with new range clock.	
		12.30pm	40 rounds at front line C14 a 3½.4 retaliation for hostile shelling	
		4.30pm	10 in w14a 5½.6	
		5pm	18 rds)	
		6.15pm	16 rds) C8C 20.55. Trench junction in conjunction with heavy artillery	Elen O
		6.55pm	12 rds)	
	27/4/16	7.10pm 8.10pm	20 rounds C14 a1.7 – C14 a 3½.4 in retaliation for hostile bombardment	Elen O
	28/4/16	4.15pm	12 rounds C4 a v.C	Pll
			nil	

WAR DIARY or INTELLIGENCE SUMMARY

Army Form C. 2118

of 3/2/49 Bde R.F.A.

(Erase heading not required.)

Place	Date	Hour	Summary of Events and Information	Remarks and references to Appendices
AVELUY B25B6.6	29/4/16		Nil	Nil
	30/4/16	10.20am	1/20 rounds C.14 a 32.4 retaliation for tooth shelling — much damage done —	Nil
		4.12 noon		
		4.30pm	fired 27 rounds on CRESAR'S NOSE to cover T.M.'s firing on that salient	

Andrew Scott
Comdg P/49 R50 R.F.A.

30/4/16

WAR DIARY of **C/119 Bde R.F.A** **Army Form C. 2118**
or
INTELLIGENCE SUMMARY
(Erase heading not required.)

Map Ref. 28 N.W. 2 Belgium

Place	Date	Hour	Summary of Events and Information	Remarks and references to Appendices
In the Fields	1.11.16		Daily Routine. Improving drainage of Battery Position & constructing new Cookhouse & generally improving wagon line	—
	2.11.16		Improving drainage. Constructing new Cookhouse & strengthening roof of No 2 Gunpit.	—
	3.11.16		Improving drainage. Completing new Cookhouse & completing strengthening roof of No 2 Gunpit & work commenced on new dug-out No 4 81st Bn Gunners. Sgt admitted to Hospital (injured)	—
	4.11.16		Improving drainage of work proceeding on new dug-out. Gnr Price & Corsin returned to duty from a course at Artillery School.	—
	5.11.16		6 nights march-on granted 10 days extra leave on account of ill health. Drainage & constructing new dug-out. Car drivers detached to Bde Hqrs. Gnr Meadows Gnr detached to depot school for a course of Instruction. 1 L——Horse died.	—

Army Form C. 2118

WAR DIARY
or
INTELLIGENCE SUMMARY

(Erase heading not required.)

Instructions regarding War Diaries and Intelligence Summaries are contained in F.S. Regs., Part II. and the Staff Manual respectively. Title Pages will be prepared in manuscript.

Place	Date	Hour	Summary of Events and Information	Remarks and references to Appendices
	6.11.16		Work continued on new dug out & drainage. 4 & 56 P.S Garrison to Hospital.	
	7.11.16		Work continued on new dug out & on drainage. 2 L. O stores posted from Rouen ord depot.	
	8.11.16		Work continues on dug out & on drainage.	
	9.11.16		Work continued on dug out & drainage. 2286 Dvr Lewis J— to Lent Hospital, Rich.	
	10.11.16		Work continues on new dug out & drainage.	
	11.11.16		Work continues on new dug out & drainage. 42 Sergt Partridge returned from leave. 4256 D/S Harrison reported from Hospital.	
	"			
	12.11.16		Work continues on new dug out & drainage. No 3160 Gnr Huxton G detached to Signal School for a course in visual signalling. No 24150 Sergt Saunders H.C. detached to 2nd Army Artillery School for a course of Instruction.	

Army Form C. 2118

WAR DIARY
or
INTELLIGENCE SUMMARY
(Erase heading not required.)

Instructions regarding War Diaries and Intelligence Summaries are contained in F.S. Regs., Part II. and the Staff Manual respectively. Title Pages will be prepared in manuscript.

Place	Date	Hour	Summary of Events and Information	Remarks and references to Appendices
Ypres Sector	13.11.16		Work continued on new dug out & on drainage system	
	14.11.16		Work continued on new Dug-out & on drainage system. No 7443 Sergt Spurway RE proceeded on leave to England. No 2203 Corpl Gibson R. to Hospital for Dental Treatment	
	15.11.16		Work continued on dug out & drainage	
	16.11.16		Work continued on dug out & drainage. No 2586 Pte Lewis D. discharged from Hospital	
	17.11.16		Work continued on Dug out & drainage. No 3176 Pte Evans J.S. proceeded on a course of Divisional Gas School	
	18.11.16		Work continued on new dug out & drainage	
	19.11.16		Work continued on new dug out & drainage. No 3880 Gnr Bracey D. posted from 38th D.A.C. 1 L. horse posted to mobile Veterinary Hospital	
	20.11.16			

1875 Wt. W593/826 1,000,000 4/15 J.B.C. & A. A.D.S.S./Forms/C. 2118.

WAR DIARY
or
INTELLIGENCE SUMMARY

Army Form C. 2118

Place	Date	Hour	Summary of Events and Information	Remarks and references to Appendices
Iales Field	21.11.16		Work continued on New Dug out & drainage	
			2/Lt Bones, R.A. detached to 6/22 for a course of Instruction	
			2/Lt G. A. Trafford C/22 attached for a course of Instruction	
			3420 Dvr Hopes E.A. posted to 1st Texas Brigade (B.U.)	H.S.
			No 596447 S. Jones P.I. transferred to the Base — under age	
			3 names submitted to Brigade office for future leaves.	
	22.11.16		New dug out completed, work on drainage proceeding.	H.S.
			No 158 Gnr Stormer J. to hospital for Dental treatment.	
	23.11.16		Drainage attended to	H.S.
			Capt W. M. Matheson struck off strength of Battery	
	24.11.16		Drainage attended to	H.S.
			No 2203 Corpl Green returned from hospital	
			No 158 Gnr Stormer S.A. returned from hospital	

WAR DIARY
or
INTELLIGENCE SUMMARY

Army Form C. 2118

Place	Date	Hour	Summary of Events and Information	Remarks and references to Appendices
In the Field	25/11/16		Improving position generally	
	26/11/16		Improving position generally. No 21716 Som Evans R.J. Richards from a course at Divisional Gas School	
	27/11/16		Improving position Generally. No 24150. Sergt Alexander J.C. returned from Artillery School	
	28/11/16		Improving Position. New oven constructed. Battery position inspected by G.O.C. Division & G.O.C. R.A. Lieut Myatt proceeded on leave. No 41351 Dvr. Blake A.J. proceeded on leave.	
	29/11/16		Improving position generally	
	30/11/16		Improving position generally	

Leonard Horwood Lieut R.F.A.
for O.C. Coy. C/119

Army Form C., 2118

WAR DIARY
or
INTELLIGENCE SUMMARY
(Erase heading not required.)

Instructions regarding War Diaries and Intelligence Summaries are contained in F. S. Regs., Part II. and the Staff Manual respectively. Title Pages will be prepared in manuscript.

Place	Date	Hour	Summary of Events and Information	Remarks and references to Appendices

1875 Wt. W593/826 1,000,000 4/15 J.B.C. & A. A.D.S.S./Forms/C. 2118.

WAR DIARY
INTELLIGENCE SUMMARY
D/119 (How) Battery R.F.A.

Army Form C. 2118.

Hour, Date, Place	Summary of Events and Information	Remarks and references to Appendices
Battery H.Q. at GHENT COTTAGES BRIELEN Right Section in action at :- O.22.d.90.15. Left Section in action at :- O.22.d.4.3. OP at THIN COTT (Touch) B.19.b.93.3	Nov. 1. Good light front observation throughout the day. Crew TM's fired about 30 rounds between 10 and 11 am. Swinging on hostile retaliation; each 1 light and 1 medium TM. Fire on which the battery have fired MINNIE retaliation under orders from Jeff Group. At 3 pm, one L and 12 m. Howitzer opened fire on VON MOLTKE Redoubt near PILCKEM. Fire concentrating about 4.30 pm. About 5 hy enemy retaliated on CANAL BANK and Trenches in C1c south 10.5 cm howitzer and some hy field batteries (77m) at 5.15 pm and 5.55 pm. The Battery fired under gas helmets in retaliation.	Nov 1
	2. A quiet night. Work on rear section boarders continued. Spaces between double rows picketted in and cemented in front of huts to stop possibility of shell penetrating between roofs.	Nov 2
	3. Registered with aeroplane. Right TM fire of Germans on VON MOLTKE for which we retaliated. Right TM fire by Germans. Dwr Haws fired on afternoon drawing heavy retaliation for which we retaliated.	Nov 3
	4. Slight activity by TM's we retaliated.	Nov 4
	5. Quiet day. Hostile working parties dispersed.	Nov 5
	6. N.? Howrs posted to the Battery which is now up to strength. Considerable hostile fire on our front line about 8 am. Trenches bombarded also retaliation and about 10.45 am bombarded VON MOLTKE Redoubt, lt.PICKEM in conjunction of shoot by 2nd Lieut Hourtzgere Jeff Houtie Sec.	Nov 6
	7. Heavy rain.	Nov 7
	8. Quiet day. Capt L.R. Page RFA to England on case of influenza avoiding Command	Nov 8

BATT. 119TH BRIGADE R.F.A.

Army Form C. 2118.

WAR DIARY
or
INTELLIGENCE SUMMARY.
(Erase heading not required.)

Instructions regarding War Diaries and Intelligence Summaries are contained in F.S. Regs., Part II. and the Staff Manual respectively. Title pages will be prepared in manuscript.

D BATT. 119TH BRIGADE
No.....
Date.....
R. F. A.

Hour, Date, Place	Summary of Events and Information	Remarks and references to Appendices
Mon 9	Engaged entire battery 9.30am MINNIE retaliation from GROVE trench during day. BOMBARD also received.	
10	About 1.30pm about 10-110 our FGC in neighbourhood of L.2.c.6.7. About 6 heavies and none very near	
	Mon. fired about 30 minnies with TM and scabo and 18 pairs of front line [?] by a fortnight. Bombardment reported afterwards by infantry.	
11	Misty and quiet. Retaliated once for MINNIE and fired once at working party at PICKEM. Ordered today to fire on circles of group only	
12	Misty day. Quiet. Car. Laugh inspected the bootees.	
13	10am Retaliated twice for Minnies. Very foggy morning. Non. GOC Division, GOC RA, and Col. Laugh. inspected [?] pits and huts. Had nothing to complain of. Fought good in afternoon	
14	11.15am shot at MAUSER OBY. Bombarded front line in afternoon four guns engaged in enemy?	
15	8 pm Guns and Howitzers in forward section to replace two (3P = 2P) which had snake battery now constituted	A 1035 NCF 1915
		B 1251
		C 604 1916
		D 305 1911
		G Circa 1915
16	7pm-6.7pm fired 200 rounds front line Crost. L G Circa 7 and expected for about attack. Very cold. Engaged two hostile battery during morning	
17	11.30am 100 minnies on front line as say before or preparation for about	

WAR DIARY or INTELLIGENCE SUMMARY

Army Form C. 2118.

(Erase heading not required.)

Instructions regarding War Diaries and Intelligence Summaries are contained in F.S. Regs., Part II and the Staff Manual respectively. Title pages will be prepared in manuscript.

D BATT. HON. BRIGADE
No. ....
Date ....
R. F. A.

Sheet 3

Hour, Date, Place	Summary of Events and Information	Remarks and references to Appendices
Nov 17. 6.30pm	200 rounds in preparation for raid to 7.30pm. 300 rounds in raid on HGH (COMPANY) REDOUBT. Very successful, took 36 prisoners.	Ntd.
18.	Very wet and cold. Fired 13 rounds at Hooge Battery Front.	Ntd.
19.	Conference Group Commander. Concentrations on the enemy front.	Ntd.
20.	Quiet day. Shot new Canon at trench Jar.	Ntd.
21.	Foggy. Not engaged.	Ntd.
22.	Foggy. Not engaged.	Ntd.
23.	Lieut Wolfenden RFA to England on leave. (Lieut Ames) from absence Command. Registered new MINNIE trees (CRATERS SUPPORT). Registration of new pieces on CANON FARM. Enlarge 1 good on enemy front line at Cnd 95.A.4.	Ntd.
24.	Misty. No hostile fire of any kind.	Ntd.
25.	Heavy mist. Not engaged.	Ntd.
26.	Good shooting day. Destroyed new work on FERME FLAREUIL. Scarp to redoubt on front line C9d 95.11. registering for Group shoot on Trench 70. (FCZ Z1 serviceable from OP + 100x to front gun Rounded parapet of C9d 95.1A. MINNIE-EALING (2) and BOMBARD by Group orders. Also knocked down No 2, 1 during evening fired on Salvos by Group orders at CCZ Z1. Shot one at 9.20pm knocked hostile retaliation which led to MINNIE-EALING Fire.	Ntd.
27.	Aeroplane registration of Hooglee Galleny No 9 D of (between 3pm + 3.35pm). BOMBARD (2) and MOLTKE; at 7.30pm Group ordered Salvo on front line CA9 Z1. Z1. Enemy shelled heavily with TMS and No 5 and Hos. MINNIE—EALING (2) and MINNIE 8 & 8.35pm Section fire 20 secs on NGT LINES.	Ntd.

Army Form C. 2118.

WAR DIARY
or
INTELLIGENCE SUMMARY.
(Erase heading not required.)

Hour, Date, Place	Summary of Events and Information	Remarks and references to Appendices
Nov 27	Quiet until 9.20 when we fired by Group Order at TRENCH & TRAMWAY Cyas5 96. One howitzer to 10M for overhaul.	Windy.
28	Foggy	Windy
29	Foggy	Windy
30	Foggy and very cold. JNF apparently from neighbourhood of FARM 4 shelled that place. BOM39Ad	Windy

Commanding D. Battery
119th Brigade R.F.A.

WAR DIARY
or
INTELLIGENCE SUMMARY

(Erase heading not required.)

Army Form C. 2118

Map Ref - Sheet 28 Belgium
119th Brigade R.H.A.

Place	Date	Hour	Summary of Events and Information	Remarks and references to Appendices
TROIS TOURS	1.12.16 to 2.12.16		A very quiet day on the whole front. About 11.50 p.m. on the 1/12/16 the enemy opened a very heavy Trench Mortar Bombardment on the front line and support trenches of the Rfl Battalion between points C7.c.1.7 to C.13.c.8.2. Our 18 pdrs and 4.5 Hows. retaliated and apparently broke down a raid. Fire ceased about 12.45 am on 2/12/16	W.T.C
"	3/12/16		Hostile Artillery activity was fairly large in the morning. A Direct hit was obtained on a gun pit of D/119 by a 10.5 Howitzer slightly wounding one gunner. No other casualties to personnel or equipment	W.T.C
"	4/12/16		Our Artillery fired very little.	W.T.C
"	5/12/16		More active than usual along the whole front. The enemy appeared to be registering. We replied in a corresponding manner	W.T.C
"	6/12/16		Considerable promiscuous shelling throughout the whole area by enemy 77 mm guns and 4.2 Hows. Our Artillery retaliated lightly	W.T.C

Army Form C. 2118

WAR DIARY
or
INTELLIGENCE SUMMARY

(Erase heading not required.)

Map ref Sheet 28 Belgium 1/40,000

Place	Date	Hour	Summary of Events and Information	Remarks and references to Appendices
TRDIS TPERS	7/12/16 to 8/12/16		Nothing to report. Very thick fog and mist	WX
"	9/12/16		On the morning of 9th. at 1am. We carried out a small enterprise viz Artillery covering the fire of Stokes Mortars in the KRUPP SALIENT at C11/4 & Central. Very little retaliation on part of Enemy. During the day considerable Activity on both sides.	WX
"	10/12/16		Had a good amount of retaliation work to do as Enemy fired considerably on our Trenches and Support lines apparently registering. In the early part of the night the appeared to be testing the S.O.S. among ments. We retaliated	type
"	11/12/16 to 12/12/16		Very cloudy & misty. Weather unfavourable to see.	WX

WAR DIARY or INTELLIGENCE SUMMARY

Army Form C. 2118

Map Ref. Sheet 27 and 28
Hazebrouck 5A

Instructions regarding War Diaries and Intelligence Summaries are contained in F.S. Regs., Part II. and the Staff Manual respectively. Title Pages will be prepared in manuscript.

Place	Date	Hour	Summary of Events and Information	Remarks and references to Appendices
Trois Tours	13.12.16		Some activity on both sides	WDC
"	14.12.16		Received orders to proceed to HOUTKERQUE to Rest Billets. The 186th Brigade being ordered to relieve the 119th Brigade in action.	WDC
"	15.12.16		Half relief completed during night of 14/15. Bty transport lines moved to new take up route march.	WDC
HOUTKERQUE	16.12.16		Relief completed remaining personnel going to rest area by lorries. Brigade Headquarters at E.20 b 9.9 Sheet 27 (A Bty E 14 c 1.2) B By - E 8 c 1.8) C Bty E 2 c 6.6) D E 3 c 0.4).	WDC
"	17.12.16		Nothing to report.	
"	18.12.16		Orders received to march to training area at WISSANT (2 days march) 3 miles E.N.E of Cape Grinez and to start on the 19th inst.	
March	19.12.16		Left HOUTKERQUE at 10.a.m, for Ledergem & Wulverdinghe, via Esquelbecq Wormhoudt- the Brigade was passed the C. in C (Sir Douglas Haig) & Lieut Genl Sir Harbert Plumer, the Corps Commander & Genl Western	

1875 Wt. W593/826 1,000,000 4/15. J.B.C. & A. A.D.S.S./Forms/C. 2118.

Army Form C. 2118

HAZEBROUCK 572.
CALAIS 13

WAR DIARY
or
INTELLIGENCE SUMMARY
(Erase heading not required.)

Instructions regarding War Diaries and Intelligence Summaries are contained in F.S. Regs., Part II. and the Staff Manual respectively. Title Pages will be prepared in manuscript.

Place	Date	Hour	Summary of Events and Information	Remarks and references to Appendices
On route	19/9/16	11.50 a.m.	The C in C. got into his Motor car, and after meeting the Brigade, congratulated him & his Brigade without the condition of the horses & the appearance of the troops. The Brigade arrived eventually at LEDERZEELE & WULVERDINGHE & B.H.Q. was established at the former village.	WULVERDINGHE
	20/9/16	10.0 a.m.	The Brigade continuing its journey left LEDERZEELE at 10.0 a.m. for NORDAUSQUES, where it arrived at 12.55 p.m. B.H.Q. established at NORDAUSQUES.	
	21/9/16	8.30 a.m.	The Brigade left NORDAUSQUES for WISSANT via ARDRES and GUINES - at 8.30 a.m. and arrived at WISSANT 4.0 p.m. Brigade Headquarters East of the village.	
WISSANT	22/9/16		Very wet rainy weather & much rain. Notwithstanding the preliminary day's training was satisfactory. Officers driving and riding drill - N.C.O's rides etc.	
"	23/9/16		Rainy nearly all day & blowing a gale, so that circumstances were again noted to continue training. Section Gun drill, section driving drill, Officers rides & driving drill. 2/Lt. J. Ennui instructed in riding. Lieut W.D. Cook instructed in driving - So lectures in the evening under Battery Commanders.	

Wt. W 593/826 1,000,000 4/15 J.B.C. & A. A.D.S.S./Forms/C.2118.

Army Form C. 2118

WAR DIARY
or
INTELLIGENCE SUMMARY
(Erase heading not required.)

III CALAIS 13
HAZEBROUCK 5A

Place	Date	Hour	Summary of Events and Information	Remarks and references to Appendices
WISSANT	24/12/16		Another day of action training as the snow turns as the frozen day but under better climatic conditions.	
"	25/12/16		Xmas day — no work done.	
"	26/12/16		Battery training — Field manoeuvres	
"	27/12/16		Battery training. Battery gun drill, manoeuvres.	
"	28/12/16		Brigade Training, manoeuvres. Reconnaissance up positions as to cover SOC.RA 38th Div was present during the day.	
"	29/12/16		Brigade training again similar programme to that of preceding day. Re-during.	
"	30/12/16			
"	31/12/16		Brigade begins its march from WISSANT. Arrives at NORDAUSQUES BHQ established in the village.	
"	31/12/16		Colonel P.J. Parkinson DSO R.F.A. leaves for England on 17 days leave. The Brigade commanded by Capt. E.P. Wyse in his absence.	

W.W.W.
Lieut. Col. R.F.A.

Army Form C. 2118.

WAR DIARY
or
INTELLIGENCE SUMMARY

(Erase heading not required.)

Instructions regarding War Diaries and Intelligence Summaries are contained in F.S. Regs., Part II. and the Staff Manual respectively. Title Pages will be prepared in manuscript.

Place	Date	Hour	Summary of Events and Information	Remarks and references to Appendices
In the field	1/9/16		Improving position generally	
do	2/9/16		do. do	
do	3/9/16		No 90th Corpl Dudley E.J. proceeded to 2nd Army Artillery School for a course of Instruction. No 596 A/Bom Gardener L. proceeded on leave to England Improving position generally.	
do	4/9/16		Howitzer No 1274 returned from I.O.M. workshop Improving position.	
do	5/9/16		2nd Lieut f.P. Mackenzie joined from B Battery, 2 H.A. cowduroi No 1st 30112 D. S Fraser H. posted from 38th D.A.C. Howitzer No 861 withdrawn from action sent to I.O.M workshop for overhauling. Improving position generally.	

2449 Wt. W14957/M90 750,000 1/16 J.B.C. & A. Forms/C.2118/12.

Army Form C. 2118.

WAR DIARY
or
INTELLIGENCE SUMMARY

(Erase heading not required.)

Instructions regarding War Diaries and Intelligence Summaries are contained in F.S. Regs., Part II. and the Staff Manual respectively. Title Pages will be prepared in manuscript.

Place	Date	Hour	Summary of Events and Information	Remarks and references to Appendices
In the Field	6/12/16		Improving position generally. No 3090 Dvr Chadwick W. admitted to Hospital (Sick) I.D. Horse to mobile Vet Hospital	
do	7/12/16		Improving position generally	
do	8/12/16		No 4814 Dvr Thomas J.L. struck off Strength. Improving position, work commenced on New Dugout.	
do	9/12/16		Work continued on New Dugout. 2nd Lieut. S.R. Bowes proceeded on leave to England. No 1019 Sergt Jones C. proceeded on leave to England. No 2283 Dvr J Davies admitted to Hospital (Sick) No 337 Gnr Steel D admitted to Hospital (Sick)	
do	10/12/16		Lieut H.L. Ibgett returned from leave in England. Work continued on New Dug-out	

Army Form C. 2118.

WAR DIARY
or
INTELLIGENCE SUMMARY
(Erase heading not required.)

Instructions regarding War Diaries and Intelligence Summaries are contained in F. S. Regs., Part II. and the Staff Manual respectively. Title Pages will be prepared in manuscript.

Place	Date	Hour	Summary of Events and Information	Remarks and references to Appendices
In the field	11/7/16		No 4354 Sergt. J. Blake returned from leave in England. Work continued on New Dugout.	[sgd]
do	12/7/16		Work continued on New Dugout	[sgd]
do	13/7/16		Howitzer No 864 returned from I.O.M. workshop	[sgd]
do	14/7/16		No 34190 Dvr Chadwick W. returned to duty from hospital. Work continued on New Dug-out	[sgd]
do	15/7/16		Lieut R.F Burrill proceeded on leave to England. No 477 Corpl Saulin W. proceeded on leave to England. Battery withdrawn from action & rejoined Brigade.	[sgd]

H. Ryett Kent
R.F.A.
CO. C BG. "C" BTY,
219th BRIGADE, R.F.A.

2

Lieut Ramsby will meet billeting parties on arrival at WISSANT.

(6) "A" Battery will detail an officer to remain in rear in charge of all baggage & supply wagons

(7) Refilling point tomorrow 21st inst in NORDAUSQUES at 8.0am.

(8) ACKNOWLEDGE.

M Dearby Lieut R+a.
Adjt. 119 Brigade R+a.

Copy No 1 filed	Copy No 4. A Bty	Copy No 7 DBty
" 2 RA.	" 5 B "	" 8 Warding
" 3 BHQ	" 6 C "	" 9 "

(6) Batteries will line up their own billeting before leaving.

(7) All Baggage and Supply wagons to march in rear of the column under an Officer or responsible N.C.O. detailed by D/119.

(8) ACKNOWLEDGE

J. M^c____ Lieut R.F.A
Adjt 119 Bde
R.F.A.

OPERATION ORDER Nº 3 by
Lieut-Col. P.J. Paterson D.S.O., R.F.A.
Commanding 119 Bde R.F.A.

Headquarters 19/12/16 Tuesday

(1) In continuance of 38th Divn Artillery Operation Order Nº 43.
(2) The Brigade will march from LEDERZEELE and WULVERDINGHE to NORDAUSQUES on the 20th inst. Starting Point Cross Roads just above the "a" in "le Bostaks" and just S.W. of WULVERDINGHE. Time 10 a.m.
(3) Route:- WATTEN:- EST MONT: thence main road to NORDAUSQUES.
(4) Order of march:- B.H.Q., D.C.B.A.
(5) Billeting parties to meet Lieut. Ransley at starting Point above mentioned at 8 a.m. Forage & Rations to be carried for the day.

(1)

Copy No 9

Operation order No 4 by Lieut-Col
P.J. Paterson DSO RFA Commanding
119th Brigade RFA.

Headquarters. Wednesday 20 December 1916
Ref. sheets. 5A & No 13. Calais 1/100,000.

① In further reference to 38th Divn Artillery
Operation order 170/43 dated 18th Decr 1916.

② The Brigade will march to WISSANT
from NORDAUSQUES on the 21st inst.
Starting point Cross-roads North west
of NORDAUSQUES, and just above the
"U" in LA RECOUSSE Time 8.30am

③ Route: ARDRES, GUINES, PIHEN,
WISSANT.

④ Order of march BHQ. B. A. C. D
batteries.

⑤ Billeting parties consisting of one
officer and one man from each
Battery to leave the starting point
above mentioned at 7.0am.

S E C R E T.   Copy No. 8

"MARCH" ORDER NO. 2 BY LIEUT., COL., P.J.PATTERSON D.S.O.,
R.F.A., COMMANDING 116th BRIGADE R.F.A., 26th DIV., ARTILLERY.

Headquarters   Havre   10th December 1915.

Reference Sheet No. and No. 16 CARTE 1/100,000:

(1)   In further reference to attached 26th Div., Artillery
        Order No. 4?, and Administrative Instructions to accompany O.C.
        Order No. 4.

(2)   116th Brigade will proceed by march route from
        MONTREUIL on the 10th December. Starting point Cross Roads
        N.W. of the "R" in MONTREUIL on the main road to MARTEL.
        Time 10 a.m.

(3)   Route :- MONTREUIL, MARTEL, ...,
        MESNIERES, ST-SOUPLE, VOLFRINGHOVE.

(4)   Order of march, R.H.Q., "A", "B", "C" and "D" Batteries.

(5)   Billeting parties, consisting of one Officer or an
        N.C.O. (the former if possible) and one man from each Battery,
        to meet Lieut., Langley outside the Brigade Headquarters Office
        at 7.45 a.m. 10th inst.   Horses and rations to be carried for
        the day.

(6)   "C" Battery will detail the senior N.C.O. (not below
        the rank of B.Q.M.S.) to be left behind at MARTEL to take over
        all Brigade supplies.   This N.C.O. must be informed of the
        route his Brigade is to take, time of starting, etc.

(7)   The Billeting parties will meet the r'units at the
        Cross Roads in VOLFRINGHOVE, and will guide them to their
        Billets.

(8)   ACKNOWLEDGE.

                                        [signature]
                                                Lieut., R.F.A.
                                        Adjutant 116th Brigade R.F.A.

Copy No. 1 Filed.
"   " 2 R.A., H.Q.
"   " 3 A-116.
"   " 4 B-116
"   " 5 C-116
"   " 6 D-116
"   " 7 War Diary.
"   " 8 "

SECRET.   Copy No ...9...

OPERATION ORDER NO. 1. BY LIEUT., COL., P.J.PATERSON D.S.O.,
R.F.A., COMMANDING 119th BRIGADE R.F.A., 38th DIV., ARTY.

Headquarters   Wednesday   13th December 1916.

(1)   In accordance with Operation Orders No. 41, 42,
and Correction G.S. 1241 and F.A. 4321 (Lorries) on completion
of the first relief night 14th/15th inst., all personnel then
relieved and all personnel, horses and vehicles in wagon lines
will march to the new area as detailed under G.S.1241, dated
12.12.1916.

(2)   Starting Point L.5.d.6.6. where Switch Road joins
POPERINGHE - PROVEN Road.
            Time 8.30 a.m.

(3)   Order of march :-
            B.H.Q., "A", "B", "C" and "D" Batteries.
Head of Column to pass starting point at 8.30 a.m. 15th inst.
Units will ensure that they are at the Starting Point in time
to take up their order of march.

(4)   Route :- Switch Road, Cross Roads L.4.b., WATOU,
HOUTKERQUE.

(5)   Batteries, on arriving at the Church in HOUTKERQUE,
will branch off to their various billeting areas.

(6)   Immediately on arrival in billets, Batteries will
report to B.H.Q. - E.20.b.9.9. Sheet 27 - by orderley, the
time of arrival in billets.

(7)   Acknowledge.

                                         Lieut., R.F.A.
                                 Adjutant 119th Brigade R.F.A.

Copy No. 1 Filed.
   "   2 A.119
   "   3 B.119
   "   4 C.119
   "   5 D.119
   "   6 Lieut., Ransley.
   "   7 R.S.M.Reed.
        8 War Diary
        9 "

WAR DIARY
or
INTELLIGENCE SUMMARY

(Erase heading not required.)

Army Form C. 2118

38

Vol / July Hazebrouck 5A
Month: Jan. 1917
119th Brigade R.F.A.

Place	Date	Hour	Summary of Events and Information	Remarks and references to Appendices
NORDAUSQUES	1st Jan. 1917	9.30 a.m.	The 119th Brigade continuing its march from the training area at WISSANT arrived at LEDERZEELE from NORDAUSQUES at 2.0 p.m. The R.H.Q. were established in the village.	
	2nd	8.30 a.m.	Continuing the Brigade marched at 8.30 from LEDERZEELE to HERZEELE whence it arrived at 3.0 p.m.	
	3rd		Work started on billets, horse lines etc.	
	4th 13th		Brigade at HERZEELE.	
	14th		The reorganisation of the Brigade completed. The 119th Brigade R.F.A. becoming 119th Army Brigade R.F.A. but remaining attached to the 38th Division. C Battery of howitzers is split up, one section joining D/121 Brigade and one section joining D/122 Brigade, thereby completing them to 4.5" howitzer batteries. B/119 Brigade becomes C/119 Brigade and No. 3 section Divisional Ammunition Column becomes 119th Brigade Ammunition Column. The Brigade now consisting of 3 6/18 pdr batteries and one howitzer battery and a Brigade ammunition column.	

Army Form C. 2118

Map 14. Sheet 27 & 28.

WAR DIARY
or
INTELLIGENCE SUMMARY
(Erase heading not required.)

Place	Date	Hour	Summary of Events and Information	Remarks and references to Appendices
HERZEELE	Jan. 15		Nothing to report.	
	16th		Orders received that the 39th Div: Artillery plus 119th Army Bde R.F.A. is to relieve 39th Div: Artillery in the left section. Lieut-Col. P.J. Patison returned from leave in England & assumed command of the Brigade.	
	17/18		On the night 17/18th each Battery relieved one section	
	18/19		On the night 18/19th remainder of sections relieved. Brigade headquarters moved up to the line.	
	19th		Relief complete at 8.0am. Colonel P.J. Patison D.S.O. in command of the left group at B.S.C.8.6. (Elverdinghe) Group comprised 8-14-18pdr & 2 howitzers - C Battery 119th Army Bde - A Battery 121 Brigade - Section C Battery 122 Bde - Section howitzers - D Battery 119 Army Bde R.F.A.	
	19th		119th Army Brigade R.F.A. wagon lines relieved 55th Division wagon lines as follows:- A Battery took over from B/277 - 119 B.M.A. remained occupied the same wagon lines as A Battery. L.3.6.8.9. B Battery 119 Bde - A 277 Bde at L.15.C.4.1. D Battery - A 275 Bde at L.3.b.9.9.	
	20th to 22nd		The front was very quiet. Hostile Artillery practically silent all the time.	

Army Form C. 2118

WAR DIARY
or
INTELLIGENCE SUMMARY
(Erase heading not required.)

Place	Date	Hour	Summary of Events and Information	Remarks and references to Appendices
Elverdinghe	23/25		Hostile artillery more active. We retaliated strongly for enemy's shelling.	
"	26		Hostile T.M's and also more active than usual. There was very little artillery activity on either side. We carried out some registration during the day.	
"	27		Nothing to report. Front quiet.	
"	28		Enemy displayed more [?] activity. We retaliated & carried out some registration.	
"	29		Nothing to report.	
"	30		At 2.0 am the enemy opened a fierce bombardment of the Belgian front on the left of the "Left Group" front. We fired to support the Belgians who were raided. 11 Germans left some dead in the Belgian front line. At 12 noon the Left Group H.Qrs moved to ELVERDINGHE CHATEAU B.14.b.1.1.	
"	31		Nothing to report.	

Lieut-Col R.F.A.
Commanding 119 Army F.A. Bde.

SECRET.   Copy No. 8

OPERATION ORDER NO. 1 BY CAPTAIN F. P. WYE (M.C.) R.F.A.,
COMMANDING 119th BRIGADE R.F.A., 38th DIVISIONAL ARTILLERY.

Headquarters   Sunday   14th January 1917.

Reference Sheet 27 – 28, 1/40,000.

(1)   In continuance of 38th D.A. Order No. 46, dated 13.1.1917.

(2)   Receipts for all trench and billet stores mentioned in para. 4 of the above orders will be forwarded to this Office as soon as possible, (in duplicate) after the gun position and wagon line reliefs are completed.

(3)   Receipts for ammunition taken over will be forwarded, through Group, to R.A., 38th Division.

(4)   The Brigade Wagon Lines will march on the 19th inst., to the new wagon lines in the Forward Sector.

(5)   Order of march:- H.Q., "B", "A" and "D" Batteries.

(6)   Starting Point, Cross Roads – D.10.d.2.6., at 8.45 a.m.

(7)   The senior Officer of the party will take charge.

(8)   The Brigade Office will close here at 8 a.m. 19th inst., and open at B.8.c.8.6. at the same time.

(9)   Lieut., J.C.Griffiths, "A" Battery, will be the Officer in charge of Brigade Wagon Lines in the Forward Sector until further notice.

(10) ACKNOWLEDGE.

                              [signature], Lieut., R.F.A.
                              Adjutant 119th Brigade R.F.A.

Copy No. 1 Filed.
"   "   2 R.A., H.Q.
"   "   3 "A" Bty./119 Bde.
"   "   4 "B"   "   "
"   "   5 "C"   "   "
"   "   6 "D"   "   "
"   "   7 War Diary.
"   "   8

Copy No 8

OPERATION ORDER No 2.
by Capt. F.P.Wyc R.F.A. commanding
119 Bde. R.F.A.
Reference Map. Sheet HAZEBROUCK 5a.

1. The Brigade will march from
HORDAUSQUES to WULVERDINGHE
and LEDERZEELE on the 1st
January 1917.

2. Starting Point. Cross Roads
directly south of second S in
HORDAUSQUES. Time 9.30 a.m.

3. Order of March. –
     B.H.Q
     D.
     C.
     B.
     A.

(1)

4. Route:-
   OUEST MONT
   EST MONT
   WATTEN.

5. Billeting Parties under Brigade Orderly Officer to leave the above starting Point at 9 a.m.

6. Supply and Baggage Wagons will march in rear of the column under an Officer from B/119.

         T. P. Hays
       Capt for Lieut R.F.A.
Copy No 1. Filed   Adjt. 119 Bde R.F.A.
  "   " 2. R.A.
  "   " 3-6. A.B.C.D. Btys
  "   " 7. Lieut Kinsley
  "   " 8-9. War Diary.

6.30 p.m. 31/12/16.

OPERATION ORDER N° 3 by
Capt. F.P Wye R.F.A. commanding
119 Bde R.F.A. Copy N° 9.
Ref. Sheets HAZEBROUCK 5a.

(1) The Brigade will march to HERZEELE
from LEDERZEELE and WOLVERDINGHE
on the 2nd January 1917.
(2) <u>Starting Point</u>. Road Junction under
second K in VOLKERINCKHOVE.
Time 9.30 a.m.
(3) <u>Route</u>. ZEGGERS CAPPEL, WORMHOUDT
HERZEELE.
(4) Billeting Parties to leave above
Starting Point at 9.0 a.m.
(5) <u>Refilling Point</u>. 2nd January 7.0 a.m.
at WOLVERDINGHE.

Copy No. 1. Filed   L.J Deanlove.
    2. R.A.   Lieut. R.F.A.
    3-6. Batteries   Adjt. 119 Bde R.F.A.
    7. A. Ransley
    8-9. War Diary.

"A" Form.
MESSAGES AND SIGNALS.

Army Form C. 2121.

Prefix	Code	m.	Words	Charge	This message is on a/c of:	Recd. at	m.
Office of Origin and Service Instructions.		Sent			Date	
	At	m.		Service.	From	
	To					
	By		(Signature of "Franking Officer.")	By	

TO   RA 38 HOW

* Sender's Number | Day of Month | In reply to Number | AAA

Attached war diary — Batteries of this brigade detached from this group. Regret this was omitted with the war diary sent yesterday.

For Lieut Colte
A Weadon
119 Bde

From
Place
Time

The above may be forwarded as now corrected. (Z)

Censor. Signature of Addressor or person authorised to telegraph in his name.
* This line should be erased if not required.

WAR DIARY
or
INTELLIGENCE SUMMARY
(Erase heading not required.)

Army Form C. 2118

Place	Date	Hour	Summary of Events and Information	Remarks and references to Appendices
HERZEELE	19/11/17		Proceeded with Left Section to Battery Position at Dawson's Corner, north of Brielen, & relieved one Section of A/186.	
DAWSON'S CORNER B22C - Sheet 28 N.W. 1/20000	19/11/17		Right & Centre Sections came up from Herzeele, & relief of A/186 R.F.A. was completed - Position much deteriorated during past month through neglect - evident damage of Battery relieved.	
	19/11/17		Wagon lines moved from Herzeele to Wagon Lines vacated by 55th Division at L.3.b. Sheet 27 - Wagon Lines found to be in an extraordinarily filthy condition.	
	22/11/17		2nd Lieut ~~Thomas~~ proceeded on leave to England	
			Capt W.D. Cook returned from leave to England & took over charge of Wagon Lines.	
			Lieut J.C. Pettit the came up to Gun Position.	
	28/11/17 29/11/17		Lieut Bernasconi proceeded on leave to England. Enemy attempted raid on Right Battalion front, but was unable to leave his Trenches owing to Artillery Barrage fire. Battery fired 306 rds in the Barrage.	
	3/11/17		Weather has been extremely cold since the Battery has been in action - stand frost & some snow	

Rycroft Major
Comdg A/119 R.F.A.

Army Form C. 2118

WAR DIARY
or
INTELLIGENCE SUMMARY

of B/119 Bde R.F.A.

(Erase heading not required.)

Instructions regarding War Diaries and Intelligence Summaries are contained in F.S. Regs., Part II. and the Staff Manual respectively. Title Pages will be prepared in manuscript.

Place	Date	Hour	Summary of Events and Information	Remarks and references to Appendices
BRIELEN F.M. B.28.B.6	18/1/17	7pm	Battery in action B.28.B.6 — Relief completed 7pm	Reg 89 N.W.2 Ed. 3E Trenches 10000
	19/1/17	2:30pm 4pm	Fired 40 rounds on C.14.a.1.7 in retaliation	Ellis
		4pm–9:30pm	Battery heavily shelled by 5.9cm howrs & heavy guns — about 100 rds — Probably sound ranging. No damage done.	Ellis
	20/1/17	2:30pm	Fired 40 rds on C.14.a.1.7 } front line	Ellis
		3-4pm	" 35 " " }	Ellis
	21/1/17	9:15 am	Fired 6 rounds at working party C.14.a.2.8 3/4	Ellis
	22/1/17		Nil	Ellis
	23/1/17	10am	Fired 20 rds retal: at trench junction C.14.a.5.2 retaliation for T.M.S.	Ellis
	24/1/17	9.50am	Fired 6 rds at working party C.14.a.10.95 dispersed	Ellis
	25/1/17		Nil	Ellis
	26/1/17	2:30pm	Fired 9 rounds & dispersed working party C.14.a.1.7	Ellis
	27/1/17	12:15pm 1pm	Fired 11 rds C.14.a.10.85. Fired 40 rounds at trench junc. C.14.a.1.7	Ellis
		4:30pm –5pm	Battery heavily shelled by 15cm hows & gun — One shell landed in embrasure of front one gun out of action — one direct hit on dug out did not penetrate.	Ellis

WAR DIARY
or
INTELLIGENCE SUMMARY

(Erase heading not required.)

of 13/119 BDE RFA

Army Form C. 2118

Place	Date	Hour	Summary of Events and Information	Remarks and references to Appendices
BRIELEN FM B28 B36.6	26/1/17	4.50 am	Fired 6 rounds to disperse working party outpost line C14a 10.9.5	Ew
		12.45pm	Fired 24 rounds at front line C14 a 1.7 in retaliation	Ew
	29/1/17	3.15am	Fired 6 rounds at an observer C13 a 3.2.4 who disappeared	Ew
		4.45pm	Fired 42 rounds at front line C14 a 1.7 in retaliation	
	30/1/17	1.30am	Fired 35 rounds on Barrage BARBES TURCO and SOS CARREE	Ew
		12.30pm	Fired 35 rounds at CAESAR RESERVE trench between MAUSER ROT g	Ew
			KOLN FM — & 30 rounds enfilading CHEMIN AVENUE. (C8c)	
		3.15pm	Fired 33 rounds at front line C14 a 1.7 in retaliation.	
		3.30pm	„ 15 „ „ KOLN FM — calibration.	
	31/1/17	11 am -11.45 am	2 opts wounded at duty one TBR wounded	
			Fired 90 rounds at C14 a 1.7 in retaliation	
		12.30pm	Fired 17 rounds at observer in front line C14 a 3.5	Ew
		2.35pm	14 rounds on KOLN FM calibration	

Signed 1/2/17

[signature]
Major
Cmdg B/119 BdeRFA

Army Form C. 2118.

WAR DIARY
or
INTELLIGENCE SUMMARY.
(Erase heading not required.)

Instructions regarding War Diaries and Intelligence Summaries are contained in F.S. Regs., Part II. and the Staff Manual respectively. Title pages will be prepared in manuscript.

Place	Date 1917	Hour	Summary of Events and Information	Remarks and references to Appendices
Battery H.Q. at GHENT COTTS	January 17	2 pm.	Position of Battery Staff with Left Section Guns on Rd HERZEELE by motor bus on return to Battery Position just north of BRIELEN and relieved Section D/186 Bde R.F.A. 39th Division	A.P.M.
BRIELEN	18		Section D/172 Bde R.F.A. joined the Battery from 39th Divl Artly. our Battery being increased to 6 Howitzer Establishment and became Centre Section. Lt. W.F. Mount joined with this Section.	A.P.M.
No. 5 gun in action at B.22.d.7d.3.			Guns of the Section taken over in action at ELVERDINGHE (B.14.b.3.9) in a barn, carrying front of LEFT GROUP.	
No. 2 gun in action with remainder of Battery at B.22.d.2.5.5.			Capt L. Roberts R.F.A. sent to Rest Camp. Section began line reconnd in old position at HAMROEN on account of range amongst the horses.	Frost.
Left Section in action with Battery in full at B.22.d.m.3.	19		Right Section and remainder of Battery Staff travelled by motor bus from HERZEELE to gun position and relieved remainder of D/186 Bde R.F.A.	Frost.
O.P. TWIN COTTS Sheet 28. S.17.b.7.3.	19		Battery began line moved from HERZEELE to L.3.a.9.9. Just west of POPERINGHE - WATOU Road about 3/4 mile W of POPERINGHE and returned D/27.7.Bde. R.F.A. 55th Divn to P.P.P.P.P.P. detached Range 15/149 Bde R.F.A. 13 ins. Barn 8 and 15 pm about 100 rounds 15 cm + 12.5 cm HowitZer Shell, fell within BRIELEN FARM and GHENT COTTS, mostly East of main road.	Frost.
	20		Calibrated and refitted.	Frost.
	21		Quiet day.	Frost.

WAR DIARY
or
INTELLIGENCE SUMMARY

Army Form C. 2118.

(Erase heading not required.)

Place	Date 1917	Hour	Summary of Events and Information	Remarks and references to Appendices
Battery H.Q. at	January 17th		at 2 pm. Portion of Battery Staff with Left Section Gunners Left HERZEELE by motor lorries on return to Battery Position	A.P.H.
GHENT COTTS	18		just north of BRIELEN and relieved Section D/186 Bde R.F.A. 39th Division	A.P.H.
BRIELEN			Section D/170 Bde R.F.A. joined the Battery from 39th Divl Artly. one Battery being increased to 6 howitzers	
No 1 gun in action at B.22.d.9.55			Established and became Centre Section. Lt W.F. Maunder joined with his Section. Guns of his Section taken over in action at ELVERDINGHE (B.14.t.3.9) in a barn, carrying strength of LEFT GROUP	A.P.H.
No 2 gun in action mid-way between B.22.d.55.50			Section began Line remained in old position at HARINGE	
			Capt L. Roberts R.F.A. sent 10 lathe charge on account of mange amongst the horses.	
Left Section in ditto	19th		Right Section and remainder of Battery Staff travelled by motor bus from HERZEELE to gun position and relieved remainder of D/186 Bde R.F.A.	A.P.H.
HIS LWD by Battery in Sec 15 B.22.d.4.3	19th		Battery began fire moved from HERZEELE 15 L.3.B.9.9 gave north of POPERINGHE-WATOU Road	
O.P. TWIN COTTS B.17.8.73			about 3/4 mile W. of POPERINGHE and relieved D/277 Bde R.F.A. 55th Division Cabled and fired in enemy front line in retaliation. Lt. J.T. Cumminn R.F.A. attached from A/170 Bde R.F.A. Between 2 and 10 pm about 4 and more 15 cm & some 12.5 cm shrapnel shells fell between	A.P.H.
	20th		BRIELEN FARM and GHENT COTTS mainly Enemy rounds. Calibrated and retaliated	
	21st		Quiet day.	

WAR DIARY
or
INTELLIGENCE SUMMARY.
(Erase heading not required.)

Army Form C. 2118.

Instructions regarding War Diaries and Intelligence Summaries are contained in F. S. Regs., Part II. and the Staff Manual respectively. Title pages will be prepared in manuscript.

Place	Date	Hour	Summary of Events and Information	Remarks and references to Appendices
BRIELEN	22nd		Silenced hostile machine gun	Hand shot Ftn
	23rd		Fired several times in retaliation. Enemy artillery more active	Hand shot Ftn
	24th		Registered new night line	Hand shot Ftn
	25th		Fairly quiet day. Told to prepare to receive 15/16 ammunition. Rumours of intended enemy offensive.	Hand shot Ftn
	26		"S" Red 16" Hpr 4 ms a.m. 16 5.30 am. Ammunition dumped at gun position. Take 200 rounds per gun, instead of 300.	Hand shot Ftn
	27th		"S.15-0 F" ms a.m. 16 5.30 am. Rounds required during night. Retaliated on enemy front line. Hostile guns again more active. Fairly quiet day	Hand shot Ftn
	28th		Ammunition received	Rumours Hand shot Ftn
			Silenced 16" from 4 ms 16 5.15 am. Bombarded new enemy work near CAESAR'S NOSE during afternoon. B/119 Bde R.F.A at BRIELEN FARM shell by 15 cm howitzer about 100 rounds fell. Splinters all round Battery Billet. Telephone wires cut. No 90 Spencer R. received shell shock by shell exploding on the above his head and throwing him to the ground	Hand shot Ftn
	29th		Quiet day. S.O.S. rockets lighted by infantry	Hand shot Ftn
	30th		S.O.S. call received at 1.30 am. after 15 minutes slackened fire and rockets from	Hand shot Ftn

WAR DIARY
or
INTELLIGENCE SUMMARY.
(Erase heading not required.)

Army Form C. 2118.

Place	Date	Hour	Summary of Events and Information	Remarks and references to Appendices
BRIELEN	22nd		Silenced hostile machine gun fire	Narr Hirst
"	23rd		Fired usual bursts in retaliation. Enemy artillery more active	Narr Hirst
"	24th		Registered new night lines	Narr Hirst
"	25th		Fairly quiet day. Told to prepare to receive 4.5" ammunition. Ammunition of intended enemy offensive	Narr Hirst
"	26		"Stood to" from 4:45 am to 5:30 am. Ammunition dumped at gun position to be 1000 rounds per gun, instead of 500	Narr Hirst
"	27th		Quiet day. Shoot to plan nos. 12 to 5:25 am. Rounds received during night. Rapid fire against enemy wire. Remainder Retaliated on enemy front line	Narr Hirst
"	28th		Ammunition received. Fairly quiet day. "Stood to" from 4:45 to 5:15 am. Bombarded new enemy work near CAESAR'S NOSE during afternoon. 13/19 BOMBER at BRIELEN FARM shell by 15 cm howitzer about 180 rounds fell. Splinters all around Battery Billet. S.O.S. Lewis hand set to go forward. Received still shock by cross explosion on the ceiling. His colleague lying in the ground.	Narr Hirst
"	29th		Quiet day. S.O.S. rockets fired by infantry	Narr Hirst
"	30th		S.O.S. call received at 1.30 am off/Fz 15 rounds of shell shortened fire and our artillery fired	Narr Hirst

WAR DIARY
or
INTELLIGENCE SUMMARY.

Army Form C. 2118.

Place	Date	Hour	Summary of Events and Information	Remarks and references to Appendices
BRIELEN	30th cont		Grant turned two howitzers on 'right group' front. Stopped firing about 2.10 a.m. Snow during afternoon. 30 15" Howitz'r shells fell between forward gun and gun on the road. Hostile guns more active again. Several call for retaliation during the day. Night Quiet.	ditto
"	31st		Sited 16" in early morning. Calls for retaliation from div/arty during the morning. Wind Sthly & rly warmer Quiet - day	do.

31/1/19

F. Myer.
Comdg 2/Hy Bett R.F.A.

Army Form C. 2118.

WAR DIARY
or
INTELLIGENCE SUMMARY.
(Erase heading not required.)

Place	Date	Hour	Summary of Events and Information	Remarks and references to Appendices
BRIELEN	30 cont.		Enemy fired Two howitzer on to light grout front. Stopped firing about 2 p.m. Snipers during afternoon. 30 15 cm Howitzer shells fell between front and gun and hundred Rontile gun more active again. Several such fire and situation during the day. Night Quiet.	
"	31 st		"5/10 10" in early morning. Cells for retaliation from rine on by ebning to morning. Quiet day	

31/1/17

F.M.L
Lieut
O/c...9th Dy...H.F.A.

WAR DIARY
or
INTELLIGENCE SUMMARY.
(Erase heading not required.)

Army Form C. 2118.

119 Bde R.F.A. Vol/5

Place	Date	Hour	Summary of Events and Information	Remarks and references to Appendices
BRIELEN and ELVERDINGHE	1917 January 1st		ARTILLERY. Both sides very quiet. Major Bemish's Group about 5 am Battery started to fire but did not open. The latter 12 rounds and then Battery took part in Gas experiment of unknown nature on BOESINGHE Sector. Battery fired 30 rounds on BRIDGE STREET Northernmost from Wieltje — ARTILLERY WOOD in S.W. direction. 5 minute period into CANAL BANK (Target is fired gun very slowly towards end of shoot. Left section observed the line across of gun flash. Battery but got off 9 rounds in the 5 minute each. Centre Section at ELVERDINGHE also opened harassment fire 200 rounds on hostile by possible of road and railway, 300 yards N.E of BOESINGHE railway bridge over CANAL — Also opened on BOESINGHE SECTOR at about 5.15 6 pm barrage attached in POCEINGNE SECTOR. Battery arranged target period at during of Harassing.	F.M.
"	Jan 2nd	5/6 6 am	Enemy very active with Minen Werfer and field guns in hostile in BOESINGHE SECTOR and opposite FARM DIX-SECT (C.7.d.1.7) Sheet 28 A.M. Some retaliation in enemy communication trenches. Fired an WOOD 15" an every one firm into VIII Corps Heavy Artillery during the day — kind of fire retaliated for hostile shelling during the afternoon, and much accurate at strong points — German front line.	C/m
"	Feb 3rd	5-3.15 5.2 am	Fired 25 rounds on trenches by KRUPP SALIENT according to Wiring Group scheme. L retaliated for German activity yesterday morning. Calibrated during the day and retaliated once for 6" hostile shelling. Signed A.H. Lott Capt. Artillery Command of 119 B de R.F.A.	

WAR DIARY or INTELLIGENCE SUMMARY

Army Form C. 2118.

Place	Date	Hour	Summary of Events and Information	Remarks and references to Appendices
	Feb 5		Bad light for registration all day. Not engaged	
	Feb 6		Foggy rainy day. Not engaged	
	Feb 6 ?		Bombarded enemy trench lines on S.W. face of KAIPP SALIENT (M 16.80 - C.15.a.50.72) in cooperation with 78 var Corps Heavy Artillery and Corps Group B. Fired 200 rounds — satisfactory results	
			Retaliation by enemy comparatively small. Battery put on shrapnel	
			K9 H.I.SANDOM attached from C/119 FAB R.F.A. as wire tender	
	Feb 7		In cooperation with 78 Corps Heavy Artillery and Corps Group B. Battery destroyed concealment of hostile strong point — trench system at PILCKEM (where more reported). Several shoots of fire very satisfactory. Battery fired 200 rounds	
			MADDEN FARM. Shrouds [?] finally found very weak hostile retaliation	
	Feb 8		CENTRE section shelled with gas shell. One man slightly wounded on evacuating	
	Feb 8		Cultivated and fired a few rounds to check registration	
	Feb 9		Fired at dugouts in CAESAR SUPPORT TRENCH M 1801 [?] 80 [?] 29 rounds [?]	
			One hit side damaged	
	Feb 10		Quiet day. Observation from dugout in afternoon. Slight activity about M 17D 25,735	

WAR DIARY or INTELLIGENCE SUMMARY

Army Form C. 2118.

(Erase heading not required.)

Place	Date	Hour	Summary of Events and Information	Remarks and references to Appendices
	Feb 11th		Battery not engaged. Visibility poor.	
	Feb 12th		Enemy active with minenwerfer. Slight enemy trench mortaring of [Gl.?] mining Karlsbad	
	Feb 13th		MINNIE EATING. Seven times Registration of C.14 a.3.c. 77mm and of 10.5 cm Hows on Right Battalion Front activity	RNt of
	Feb 14th		Registered seven targets in KRUPF SALIENT in preparation for Raid	Rt of
	Feb 15th		Enemy registered Battery Billets with 77mm + 15cm. No direct hits on Billet, some slight damage, wounded. At times active & burned remaining mess. Obtained 4 direct hits on 17GE at C.14.a.24.79. Considerable damaged	Rt of
	Feb 16th		Visibility very poor all day. Twenty 5.9" + 10.5 cm in field in front of Billet	Rt of
	Feb 17th		Bombarded Front line C.14 a.2.3 & C.14 a.0.7½ 200 rounds. Considerable damage done	Rt of
	Feb 18th		At 3:19 am Bombarded Front line from 00.60.3 Switched to Support line & Barrage 1 in accordance with Opns Order 21. (Box Barrage)	Rt of
			Fired three rounds per gun at odd & frequent intervals at important trench & tramway junctions to impede infantry relief. 60 N 2n	
	Feb 19th		Continued 60. N 2n until midnight. No. 4 gun out of action from 8.5 pm until 2.30 am 20th bolt lever handle broken.	Rt of

2353 Wt. W2544/1454 700,000 5/15 D.D. & L. A.D.S.S./Forms/C. 2118.

Army Form C. 2118.

WAR DIARY
or
INTELLIGENCE SUMMARY.

(Erase heading not required.)

Instructions regarding War Diaries and Intelligence
Summaries are contained in F. S. Regs., Part II.
and the Staff Manual respectively. Title pages
will be prepared in manuscript.

Place	Date	Hour	Summary of Events and Information	Remarks and references to Appendices
	Feb 20		Night very quiet. Day very misty	Photo
	Feb 21		Not engaged	Photo
	Feb 22		Not engaged. Very Misty	Photo
	Feb 23		Not engaged. Very Misty	Photo
	Feb 24		Fired 25 rounds at an Active Hostile Battery at U.26.3/2.1	Photo
	Feb 25	8.30 am	Enemy bombarded our front line in neighbourhood LANCASHIRE FARM. Battery called upon for BOMBARD; Rate BARRAGE	Ph 61
	Feb 26"		Registered No1 Gun on New NIGHT LINE Registered No 2 No 4 on New NIGHT LINES Enemy put 11 15cm at BATTERY BILLET No direct hits 5 Bursts. Rate of Fire 1 round every 15 minutes	
	Feb 27		GROUP RETALIATION only	Photo
	Feb 28"		MISTY	Photo

[signature]
R M Moore R.F.A.
Lieut R.F.A.
Commanding D. Battery
119th Brigade R.F.A.

WAR DIARY
or
INTELLIGENCE SUMMARY

Army Form C. 2118

(Erase heading not required.)

Instructions regarding War Diaries and Intelligence Summaries are contained in F. S. Regs., Part II. and the Staff Manual respectively. Title Pages will be prepared in manuscript.

Place	Date	Hour	Summary of Events and Information	Remarks and references to Appendices
YPRES	3/2/17	2.35–4.25	FIRED MINNIE & BOMBARD. HOSTILE ARTILLERY unusually active.	1.F.W
	7/2/17		36 rounds Retaliation for MINNIES & HOSTILE SHELLING.	1.F.W
	8/2/17	12.50	FIRE seen in enemy's lines about C.13.6.8.5.8. 10 rounds fired, fire continued till 2.45 p.m.	1.F.W
	10.2.17	4.30 p.m.	77mm Battery & A.A. battery active; T.B. 45° & 37° respectively. Germans seen at C.11.a.7.2. & C.11.a.4.4.	
			6.5 rounds fired on works damaged by HEAVIES.	
	11.2.17	9 a.m.	6 Rounds on W.P., C.11.a.4.4.3; dispersed. 10.15 FIRED BOMBARD. BRIELEN SHELLED 4.5-9 p.m. about 200 sh.	1.F.W
	13.2.17		About 100 sh during the day Retaliation, MINNIE & COVERING T.Ms	2.F.W
	14.2.17		60 Rds covering T.Ms. One of our Aeroplanes brought down about BOESINGHE.	1.F.W
	15.2.17		FIRED 100 rounds on concrete EMPLACEMENT C.16.a.2.2.6. GOOD EFFECT. 150 rounds covering T.Ms & wire cutting.	1.F.W
	18.2.17	3.10 a.m.	RAID on ENEMY'S trenches I.19.14. R.W.F. 145 men went over, casualties heavy from enemy 77mm	1.F.W
			barrage on his own front line, which was unexpected. Some Germans seen in this line. No prisoners	
			or artillery barrages enemy thus line 9 C.Ts, 0 is thought to have inflicted some casualties.	1.F.W
	19.2.17	4.15–7.30	FIRED 1574 rounds. C.8 a.1.3; Caddie Pt; C.2.a.3.5.2.0; Cancer Trench; C.2.C.25 B–C.20.7.45; to impede enemy retal.	1.F.W
			FIRED as on 18th artillery, 35 rds retaliation. 11.0 a.m. Concielle Retaliation 17 mm. 1.30 a.m on WILD SKYTHON 1915	1.F.W
	20.2.17	1.50 p.m.	Our wagon line was moved from HOOTKER QGE to VICINITY of PESELHOEK.	1.F.W
	24.2.17	3.10 a.m.	FIRED 10 rounds retaliation on MAUSERCOT, GROODORDERS. at	1.F.W
	25.2.17	approx.	Enemy Raiders bunched at about C.11.a.4.2.4, inflicting some casualties. Our fire prevented	1.F.W
			caught him on his return to his own trench. 306 rounds fired.	
	26.2.17	11.30 p.m.	3 rounds fired on pumps reported at C.11.a.3.7 - at Enemy orders. Effect not known.	1.F.W
	27.2.17	10.30–11.0	FIRED 30 rounds at intervals at pumps reported above which could be clearly seen. Fire apparently	1.F.W
			driven by a motor – as traffic of Some kind occasionally appeared along tracks 36.2 day fires - retaliation	
			from Group orders. 20-30 77mm fired between 12.35-1.30 p.m. on SKYTHON. Shelling registration.	

K. Mclean
for Major
R.B.1.1.9

WAR DIARY
or
INTELLIGENCE SUMMARY

(Erase heading not required.)

Army Form C. 2118

Place	Date	Hour	Summary of Events and Information	Remarks and references to Appendices
In the Field	1/7/17		Battery Position at B.2.d.1.8	
"	6/7/17		Battery attached to Bento Group (Lieut. Col. Pringle Commanding) R.F.A.	
"			Capt. W.D. Booth R.F.A. Served in command arrived from Barton Group	
"	7-7-17		Wagon lines Capt. J.L. Griffiths R.F.A. to magazines & served command of Left half Battery whilst Capt. W.D. Booth R.F.A.	
"	9-7-17		Wagon lines were Capt. W.D. Booth R.F.A. Battery/Commander AMB Booth R.F.A. left to attend course of instruction in Lydd/Lydda. Capt W.D. Booth R.F.A. assumed Temporary command of AMB R.F.A. during Major C.A.R. Pryce's absence.	
"	18-7-17 3.19 am		Fired 883 rounds in conjunction with Raid by 14th R.W.F.	
"	27/7/17 8pm		Battery transferred from Easton Group to Pringle Group under the Command of Lieut. Col. Roushenur	

J.A.Bem Lt. M.P.

WAR DIARY.

The following should have been entered for January 26th 1917 –

"Under Orders issued by R.A. 38th Div. Operation order No 47, two reinforcing Batteries joined the Left Group 38th Div. A Battery 275 B'de and B Battery 275 B'de. The former relieving the personnel of the two guns of C Battery 122 B'de at V.21.d.1.9. and bringing four extra guns to the position. B Battery 275 B'de went into action as follows:— 4 guns C.25.d.55.60. and 2 guns C.26.d.6.1. Both batteries for enfilading purposes.

Lieut-Col- R.F.A.
Commanding 119 B'de

WAR DIARY
or
INTELLIGENCE SUMMARY.

Army Form C. 2118.

Sheets Ypres 28 N.W.

Place	Date	Hour	Summary of Events and Information	Remarks and references to Appendices
ELVERDINGHE	FEBRUARY 1st.	8.0am to 4pm	B/177 Bde relieved A 275 Bde C/180 Bde relieved B/275 Bde. In accordance with 38th Divn. Artillery Operation Order No 48 dated 30/1/17, we carried out a systematic bombardment of the German line opposite Boesinghe - A Battery /121 B'de (Battery) 119 B'de each firing 400 rounds, in conjunction with the Heavy Artillery, and D Battery 119 B'de 200 rounds. Much damage was done to the enemy trenches, especially Trenches C1, C, 2, 9. C1.d.o.4 C1.d.5½.7 and ¾.B.6.d. ½.½. The medium trench mortars also fired 256 rounds. The Germans retaliated about 4pm to 4.15pm, opening a fierce bombardment of BOESINGHE, and communication trenches in the vicinity. The hostile fire soon stopped after a very nifty from the Heavy Artillery and our batteries. In accordance with scheme we shelled the Bois 14 and Bois 15 in bursts of fire during the day. The Heavies co-operating. Stokes fire fairly active during the day. The light being foot & observation difficult there was very little Artillery fire on either side. C Battery 119 B'de was heavily shelled in the morning with Hostile Artillery was more active.	

WAR DIARY or INTELLIGENCE SUMMARY

Army Form C. 2118.

Sub 2F.N.W.

Place	Date	Hour	Summary of Events and Information	Remarks and references to Appendices
ELVERDINGHE	6 Sept	5.9.0.	Two guns were put out of action. These were withdrawn & sent to D.M.	
	7		Two others were put into position on the same night. Nothing to report.	
	8	10.8.20 11.20	The Germans were active especially in counter Battery work. The positions of B/77 and this group was heavily shelled during the morning with 4.2's and 5.9.0. About 400 rounds were put into the position altogether, and two guns were put out of action. An ammunition dump was set alight by a fire caused by a shell & some rounds exploded. One man of B/77 was killed & 3 men of B/77 wounded. The Battery adjoining B/77 was	
	9		The front was quiet. Nothing to report.	
	10 11 12		Normal.	
	13		Orders received that B/77 and C/180 go out of the line. The Battery position to be left unoccupied. One section of C/122 coming into action at the 4 gun position of C/180 at C.25.a.5.6.	

Army Form C. 2118.

WAR DIARY
or
INTELLIGENCE SUMMARY.
(Erase heading not required.)

Sheet 28 N.W.

Place	Date	Hour	Summary of Events and Information	Remarks and references to Appendices
ELVERDINGHE	Feb. 13		One section of Howitzers from D.277 Bty. to come into action with the present section of D.119 Fd. Sp. The front was again normal.	
	14			
	15			
	16			
	17		Nothing to report of interest. Occasional bursts of hostile artillery, quickly quelled by our retaliation.	
	18			
	19		We fired on these dates a good deal on the German communication trenches and searched his roads in rear, having received advice that in all probability a German relief was in progress on one or other of these days. Hostile artillery quiet.	
	20			
	21		Quiet on the front. The Germans retaliated strongly.	
	22		Nothing to report.	
	23		Observation impossible. The front was quiet – nothing to report.	
	24			
	25			
	26		Observations again impossible.	

Army Form C. 2118.

WAR DIARY
or
INTELLIGENCE SUMMARY.
(Erase heading not required.)

Shelf 28 N.W.

Place	Date	Hour	Summary of Events and Information	Remarks and references to Appendices
ELVERDINGHE	27		We carried out a little registration, but otherwise the front was very quiet.	
	28		Nothing to report.	

Arthur Corel? Lt
Officer Commdg 119th Army Bde R.H.A

www.ingramcontent.com/pod-product-compliance
Lightning Source LLC
Chambersburg PA
CBHW081532160426
43191CB00011B/1746